Other PaperStars by Jean Fritz

AROUND THE WORLD IN A HUNDRED YEARS:
   FROM HENRY THE NAVIGATOR TO MAGELLAN
BULLY FOR YOU, TEDDY ROOSEVELT!
HARRIET BEECHER STOWE AND THE
   BEECHER PREACHERS
STONEWALL
THE GREAT LITTLE MADISON
TRAITOR: THE CASE OF BENEDICT ARNOLD

JEAN FRITZ

MAKE WAY *for* SAM HOUSTON

Illustrations *by* Elise Primavera

The Putnam & Grosset Group

Library of Congress Cataloging-in-Publication Data
Fritz, Jean. Make way for Sam Houston.
Bibliography: p. Includes index.
1. Houston, Sam, 1793-1863—Juvenile literature.
2. Texas Governors—Biography—Juvenile literature.
3. Legislators—United States—Biography—Juvenile
literature. 4. United States. Congress. Senate—
Biography—Juvenile literature.
5. Texas—History—To 1846—Juvenile literature.
I. Primavera, Elise. II. Title.
F390.H84F75   1986   976.4'04'0924   [B]   85-25601
ISBN 0-698-11646-1
5 7 9 10 8 6

For two Texas friends
MARY D. LANKFORD
and
SUSAN SHERWOOD
whose enthusiasm for
Sam Houston is contagious.

My thanks to
DR. DORMAN WINFREY
for his generous and
critical assistance.

MAKE WAY *for* SAM HOUSTON

CHAPTER 1

All his life Sam Houston liked to do things in a big way or not at all. But when he was ten and eleven and twelve years old, there was nothing very big going on. The last battle of the American Revolution had been over and done. with twelve years before he'd even been born. (He'd been born on March 2, 1793.) Life had settled down to a day-in, day-out affair except perhaps for those people who lived in the West. And Sam didn't. He lived in Virginia with his mother, his four older brothers, his younger brother, and his three little sisters. His father, who was in the militia, was sometimes at home but most times he was not.

Of course Sam could have gone to school, but he saw no sense in that. He could already read and he didn't like to be told how to hold his pen and where to put his margins and such foolishness. Besides, who ever heard of anything big happening in a schoolroom? Instead he pretended to do big things. Sometimes he took down his father's second-best sword and pretended to be a Revolutionary soldier, slashing down Redcoats. Sometimes he whittled. Chipping away at a soft piece of pine, he let his mind go loose and heroic. Most often he read hero stories. His favorite hero was a Roman, Caius Marius, who started out as an ordinary boy but grew up to be a famous general. Sam especially liked the picture in his hero book of Marius when he'd been exiled from Rome by his enemies. There he was, standing all alone in his bare feet among some African ruins, but did he look beaten? Not Marius. He held his head high and smiled as if he knew he'd win out in the end. That was the way Sam would stand if he ever found himself in such a fix.

Then one day when he was thirteen everything changed for Sam. His father came home and announced that they were moving to Tennessee. Of course Tennessee was not in the Far West, but it was in the right direction and for all Sam knew, it might be Hero Country. Sam's father sold their Virginia farm for 1000 pounds, bought a new wagon for the trip, and wound up his business affairs.

And then Sam's father died. But since the Virginia farm had been sold and there were 419 acres of land waiting in Tennessee, his mother told the boys to load up the wagons. They were going anyway. And before long they were off— a five-horse wagon in the lead, a four-horse wagon following, and a string of dogs lolloping along on either side.

As it turned out, Tennessee was a fine place, but all Sam was allowed to see of it was 419 acres of unplowed, un-planted land. Sam was fourteen now, old enough to do a man's work, his brothers told him. Indeed, they never stopped telling him. Do this. Do that. Come here. Get a move on. Every time Sam ran off to read his hero books, his four bossy brothers would drag him back.

After a while his brothers gave up on Sam. He just wasn't cut out to be a farmer, they decided, so they took him to Maryville, the nearest town, and put him to work clerking in a store. That was even worse. Now Sam was at the beck and call of everyone who came into the store. All day he had to weigh potatoes, ladle out flour, count out nails, measure off yard goods. At last he could stand it no longer, so he put his hero books under his arm and ran away.

Of course he headed west. Not the Far West yet—just an island in the middle of the Tennessee River that was occupied by a band of Cherokee Indians. From all he'd heard, Indians lived in a free and easy way, which Sam figured would be a nice change.

And it was. Eventually his brothers tracked him down, but they might as well have stayed at home, tending their farm. Sam was lying under a tree reading a hero book when they found him. When they told him to get up and get moving, Sam didn't budge. When they argued, Sam waved them away. Please excuse him, he said. He was reading.

Sam stayed with the Cherokees for three years—the best years of his life, he later said. The Cherokee chief, John Jolly, took a fancy to Sam, adopted him as a son, and gave him an Indian name, The Raven. Sam learned to speak like the Cherokees, to dress like them, to hunt like them, and like them, he had his own medicine animal with special powers over his life. His was the eagle. And each year at corn-ripening time Sam joined in the Green Corn Dance, shucking away the bad in him so that he could, like all Cherokees, start life afresh.

Every once in a while Sam went back to check on civilization, but it didn't seem to improve. So after visiting with his mother and borrowing money so he could buy presents for his Indian friends, he returned to the island. By the end of three years he had piled up a debt of $100. This was a lot of money, and he understood (or he was made to understand) that he had to pay it back and soon. Perhaps by this time he was ready to give civilization another chance, but ready or not, he went back to get a job.

He had no notion, however, of becoming one hundred percent civilized. He kept his hair in a long queue, Indian fashion, down his back. And he decided that when he went to work, he wasn't going to take orders; he was going to give them. Since there were no grown people in Maryville who were interested in taking orders from nineteen-year-old Sam Houston, he opened a school. The price per student, he announced, would be $8 a term.

What a joke! people laughed. Sam Houston teaching school! He must have received his degree from the Indian University. Still, Sam did get enough pupils so that after one term he was able to pay off his debt. And that was enough teaching. What next? He still had big ideas and felt sure that he had a destiny that was waiting for him somewhere but he didn't know what it was or how to find it.

He may have thought about war because one had started in June 1812, soon after he'd begun to teach. America was fighting England because England kept butting into America's independence, interfering with American ships at sea, inciting the Western Indians against the United States. It was as if England was trying to get a toehold back on the American continent, which most Americans hoped would one day be theirs from coast to coast.

Still, it was not until March 24, 1813, that Sam actually heard the Hero Call. On that day an army recruiting party marched into Maryville, banners streaming, drums rolling. A sergeant made a patriotic speech to the crowd that gathered; then he tossed a handful of silver dollars on top of a drumhead. Any man who picked up a dollar was then and there a member of the United States Army.

Sam Houston stepped up, picked up a dollar, and dropped it into his pocket. He may have been the only one, for his friends made fun of him for enlisting as a common soldier without even trying for an officer's commission. But at least his mother knew how to give him a proper farewell. Many Americans still held on to ideas left over from the days of knighthood in Europe. A man who was fighting for his country liked to think he was also fighting for a special lady—

a sweetheart, a wife, or a mother—one who would send him off with a remembrance and brave words. Mrs. Houston gave Sam a ring with the single word *Honor* inscribed inside. (Sam wore the ring all his life.) And when Sam left, Mrs. Houston made a parting speech. "While the door of my cabin is open to brave men," she said, "it is eternally shut against cowards."

Sam would have to wait over a year, however, before he'd find out if he was brave or not. When at last he did go into battle, it was in Alabama against a tribe of Creek Indians who called themselves the Red Sticks and sided with the English. On March 27, 1814, Sam, an ensign now in charge of a platoon, was with General Andrew Jackson's army as it took its position on one side of a rampart of earth and logs stretched across a peninsula in a horseshoelike bend of the Tallapoosa River. On the other side were the Red Sticks armed with bows, spears, tomahawks, and rifles. Some Red Sticks were hiding in thickets, some concealed in a ravine covered with wood to serve as a fortress, but most were massed and ready for anyone and everyone who dared to scale the rampart. The first American to climb to the top was a Major Montgomery; he was killed on sight. The second was Ensign Sam Houston, leading his platoon and followed by the rest of the army, which did manage to go over the top, though many died on the way.

The battle broke up now into dozens of small battles with Sam in the middle of one, fighting and being fought. Suddenly an arrow shot from a thicket buried itself in Sam's groin. He reached down to pull it out but it was a barbed arrow; it didn't come out. He asked a lieutenant fighting beside him to pull it out, but though the lieutenant tried, he couldn't get it out either. The best thing for Sam to do, the lieutenant said, was to find the army doctor.

What? Quit the battle?

Sam pointed his sword at the lieutenant. Try again, he

said. So the lieutenant, bracing himself, tugged with all his might and the arrow came out but a lot of Sam came with it. The hole in him was so huge that whether he wanted to or not, Sam had to find help to stop the bleeding. A doctor plugged up the hole, and while Sam was lying on the ground, catching his breath, General Jackson stopped to ask about his injury. Sam was not to return to battle, he said.

Actually the battle was going well. The only resistance left was from the little fortress, where the Red Sticks were shooting through tiny window holes they had made. Jackson called for volunteers to take the fortress, but no one wanted to march through the onslaught of bullets pouring from those window holes. No one wanted to shoot at an enemy who couldn't be seen. So Sam, ignoring Jackson's command, got to his feet and ordered his platoon to follow. Perhaps he had read too many hero stories to do anything else. Perhaps this was the first time that Sam Houston had faced anything big enough to challenge his whole mind and his whole body and he had decided it was worth risking his life. But as soon as he came within range of those bullets, he was shot twice in the shoulder and once in the arm. When he collapsed, his platoon would go no farther. In the end Jackson did what perhaps he should have done in the first place. He had the fortress set on fire with flaming arrows.

The Battle of Horseshoe Bend was over and Sam was alive but barely so. Later Sam, who liked to talk about Destiny, may have given Destiny credit for the fact that he came through at all. Yet many times he must have wondered if Destiny was even on the job. The doctors re-dressed Sam's arrow wound and put a splint on his arm, but although they got one bullet out of his shoulder, they couldn't reach the other and decided not to try. That night when they moved the wounded from the field, they left Sam behind among the dead and near-dying. He wouldn't last the night, they said.

But he did last. The next day, along with some other survivors, he was rescued. Placed on a litter made of saplings, he was pulled over sixty miles of rough road to a wilderness fort. The other injured men were taken to a well-equipped station, but Sam seemed so near death no one wanted to cause him more pain. So he was left in the care of two militia officers, neither of whom had any medical experience.

Still Sam did not die. During the next year he was moved from place to place and two more doctors gave him up before a doctor in New Orleans finally got that bullet out of his shoulder. The wound never did completely heal and in early 1815, before he had a chance to fight again, the war was over. The Battle of New Orleans had been fought and won, and Andrew Jackson, the victorious general, was a national hero.

By this time Sam had become a lieutenant and expected to make the army his career. For the sake of the country, he said, he was glad for peace but as an officer he was disappointed. He had hoped to take part in more battles. Yet, as it turned out, Sam received an assignment that was exactly right for him. The United States was having trouble getting various groups of Cherokees to live where the government wanted them to live. A number of young men in Chief Jolly's Tennessee tribe, for instance, had signed an agreement to move west to land set aside for them in Arkansas Territory, but they had signed without approval from their tribe. And most of those Cherokees did not want to move anywhere.

Sam's job was to persuade them to go. Of course he was delighted to see his old Cherokee friends, who welcomed him and listened to him as they would listen to no other white man. And when Sam told them that they would be better off away from the white settlers, they believed him. All his life Sam boasted that unlike many white men, he never lied to Indians, and indeed, in his heart he knew that the Cherokees had little choice. New settlers were crowding into Tennessee and they not only begrudged the Indians their land, they had no intention of letting Indians, no matter how peaceful, live among them.

But if moving west was expected to solve Chief Jolly's problems, it had not solved the problems of his older brother, Chief Tah-lhon-tusky, and the Cherokees under his rule. Ten years before they had voluntarily moved west, but they had never received the money that the United States government had promised them. While Jolly's Cherokees were on their way down the Tennessee River, a delegation of Tah-lhon-tusky's tribe arrived in Knoxville to see the governor of Tennessee. They wanted to take their broken promises, they said, and lay them directly at the feet of the secretary of war in Washington. The governor told Sam Houston to go with them.

Always happy to help the Cherokees, Sam wanted to make them feel that he was truly one of them so he dressed as they did with a blanket around his shoulders and a silk turban around his head. This way, he figured, they would feel more comfortable when they entered the white man's official headquarters and appeared before the secretary of war.

John C. Calhoun was the secretary of war, an elegantly dressed gentleman from South Carolina with a fine set of manners, a set of strong opinions, and no sense of humor. But he certainly knew how to impress the Cherokees. At their first meeting he paraded his most gracious phrases, extended his most eloquent welcome, and sprinkled his talk with smooth-sounding promises. They would get down to business later, he said. Then, as he ushered the Cherokees

out of his office, he asked Lieutenant Houston to remain behind.

Alone with Sam, Calhoun dropped his fine manners as a person would toss off a coat. What, he demanded icily, did an officer of the United States Army mean by appearing before the secretary of war "dressed like a savage"?

Sam Houston had supposed that anyone with common sense could see the diplomatic intentions behind his choice of clothes, which, as far as he was concerned, needed no explanation or apology. At the moment Sam had room for only one thought: he did not like John C. Calhoun and nothing on earth would ever make him change his mind.

When a few weeks later Sam and the Cherokees journeyed back to Tennessee, the Cherokees had presents and seed corn and more promises, which at the moment seemed to satisfy them. The Cherokees had been bought off. This was a corrupt way to handle matters, the governor of Tennessee admitted, but it worked. So far, at least.

As for Sam, he had decided he could not honorably stay under the command of a secretary of war who had shown him such disrespect. On March 1, 1818, while still in Washington Sam had written and delivered a letter of resignation to the army.

Sam was twenty-five years old now and he may have wondered if he was any farther ahead in life than he'd been five years ago when he'd picked up that silver dollar from the drumhead. Actually, he was far ahead. He had become the friend of Andrew Jackson. More and more frequently he would visit the Hermitage, Jackson's Tennessee home, and in time Jackson would seem like a father to Sam. In turn, Jackson and his wife, Rachel, who had no children of their own, would welcome Sam as one of a close group of young people they liked to have around them. Jackson especially appreciated Sam's thoughtful attention to Rachel, a warm-hearted but countrified woman who felt out of place in sophisticated circles.

But Jackson not only became a father to Sam, he was a flesh-and-blood hero, a firm figure embodying a set of principles that would give substance to Sam's life. Jackson shared with Sam his vision of America—a growing country expanding westward until at last it would reach the Pacific coast. The land would be settled, subdued. Piece by piece it would rise into statehood and come into the fold of the nation. Star after star on the flag. The country would be ruled by common men and above the men there would always be the Constitution, holding the nation together. For if the United States was to survive, it must remain united. Indivisible. This was the foundation, according to Jackson, upon which all must rest.

With his whole heart Sam adopted Jackson's vision, but not only because it was Jackson's. Now he had a picture and words for what he'd called Destiny. Now when Sam felt the bigness in himself, he could feel the bigness in the United States at the same time.

Surely sometimes Andrew Jackson and Sam Houston talked of Texas. Although Texas belonged to Mexico, it wasn't much settled by anyone yet, but neither Sam nor Andrew Jackson was the kind of man to rule out possibilities. Just looking at a map, a person could see that, if nothing else, the United States would be more symmetrical if Texas were eventually to come into the Union.

CHAPTER 2

Although Sam now identified his future with that of the country, he was still interested in getting ahead on his own account. The best way to start, he figured, was to become a lawyer, but when he went to Nashville to begin his study, he was told it would take eighteen months to learn enough to pass the examination.

That was ridiculous, Sam said. He had his mind set on going up in the world and going fast. He couldn't waste eighteen months in study; he'd pass that examination in six months. And he did. Nor was that six months devoted entirely to study. He joined a dramatic club and was complimented on his performances, especially his ability to make people laugh. No one who knew Sam would be surprised at this, for he was a born actor who went through life treating the whole world as a stage. And for every part he played, he dressed for it.

In the next ten years he played so many roles that he acquired an extensive wardrobe. When he opened his private law office in Lebanon, thirty miles east of Nashville, he began sporting a plum-colored coat, fancy waistcoats, tight breeches, and a bell-crowned beaver hat. He was the very picture of success, radiating such an air of bigness that though he was listed in army records as six feet, two inches, people described him as taller until it was generally accepted that he was six feet, six inches. A straight-standing man with chestnut-colored hair and piercing, eaglelike eyes, he was, because of his looks alone, impressive, and he also talked big. When he began running for public office and speechifying, he became a master at knowing just when to apply his courtly manners, when to poke fun and work in a laugh, when to roll out the big words, and in the end how to bring a crowd around to his way of thinking. When he did well, he could feel a kind of electricity pass among the people as if they were saying, Yes—he's our man!

He was elected to one post after another: prosecuting attorney for the district of Nashville, major general of the Tennessee militia, and in 1823 with Jackson's support, he was unanimously chosen to represent Tennessee in the Congress of the United States. The first thing he did when he arrived in Washington was to buy himself a new hat, one so stylish, so elegant that a person would take for granted that the man under it was important. Then, with the hat on his head, Sam went to the empty chamber where the House of Representatives met and where he would be sitting. "I will show Mr. Calhoun," he told the chamber, "that I have not forgotten his insult."

Whenever he could, Andrew Jackson helped Sam get ahead, and Sam in turn worked hard for Jackson, who was in the Senate now and would, if all went well, be the next president of the United States. He almost made it. In 1824 Jackson received more votes than any other candidate but not the majority (two-thirds of the total vote) required to be president. The election had to be decided by the House of Representatives and it chose John Quincy Adams.

Jackson would have another chance in four years, and fortunately since Sam was reelected to Congress in 1825, he would be in Washington, able to help. Jackson would need help. He might be a hero and the choice of the people, but there were politicians, particularly in the East, who did not like him—partly because he had no formal education, partly because he was Western and therefore (in their view) rough. He was accused of being too partial to the common man and at the same time of being a tyrant. Moreover, those who were against Jackson felt so strongly, they were automatically against Jackson's friends, including, of course, Sam Houston.

Sam wrote that his friendship to General Jackson had "caused me all the enemies I have," yet he gloried "in the firmness of my attachment."

Actually, he was just doing his job when one of these enemies challenged Sam to a duel. Sam tried to get out of it, but in the end he claimed that he had no choice. The argument was over who should be postmaster in Nashville. Jackson supported one man; Henry Clay, secretary of state (and no friend of Jackson), supported another. Jackson dropped a note to Sam: "Attend to this," he said, and in the course of attending to it, Sam stated that Clay's candidate was "not a man of fair and upright character." Morcover, he was an eavesdropper.

When the "eavesdropper" sent Sam a challenge, Sam wouldn't accept it, but when the man's lawyer wanted to take on the fight himself, Sam found he could not refuse.

"If I call on you, there will be no shuffling, I suppose," the lawyer challenged.

"Try me," Sam said.

A duel, in which a man defends his honor, was another of those ideas left over from knighthood, but not one with which Sam had much dealing. Jackson, on the other hand, was an experienced duelist, quick to defend his honor, and had once killed a man for slandering his wife. Now he drilled Sam in pistol practice. If he wanted to shoot straight, Jackson advised, he should bite on a bullet while taking aim.

When the time came, Sam bit. He shot the lawyer in the groin and then worried that the lawyer wouldn't recover. After all, Sam had nothing against the man, and though he may have been glad that he wasn't the one shot, he was thankful that in the end his opponent did not die either.

Sam couldn't blame Jackson, however, for all his enemies. No one ever felt halfway about Sam Houston. They either loved him or hated him—sometimes on sight, sometimes without even a meeting, just on the basis of stories that circled around his name.

Fortunately, however, in 1827 there were enough people in Tennessee who loved Sam to put him up for governor of the state. Sam enjoyed campaigning. Traveling around the state, he celebrated at barn raisings, cheered at log rollings, feasted at barbecues. And he talked. He didn't care how long he talked; he just kept talking until he could feel the electricity run. It must have been hard to resist Sam Houston and his campaign charm, especially hard for people in Nashville on election day. On a dapple gray stallion Sam rode through the city, visiting every polling place, bowing politely to the voters as if he were acknowledging applause as he walked on a stage. Of course he was dressed for the part. In a black beaver hat, ruffled shirt, black satin vest with a bright Indian hunting shirt and red beaded sash thrown over his shoulders, he demanded attention, every inch of him. Even the embroidery on his socks was meant to be noticed.

Maybe Sam's appearance at the polls influenced the outcome; maybe not. In any case, he was elected governor. The following year Andrew Jackson was elected president and there was talk that Sam might be his successor. What else could this be but Destiny at work, lifting Sam Houston right off his feet, taking him perhaps all the way to the top? But as friends kept reminding Sam, there was one thing that he lacked. A wife. Anyone going up in the political world needed a wife. Sam was thirty-five years old now and though he enjoyed the company of what he called the "Dear Girls" and had twice come close to marrying, he had held off. Taking any kind of lifelong vow was a scary business, and though it was easy for Sam to fall in love, he was never sure if his love would last. Then he saw Eliza Allen again. He had known Eliza, the daughter of an old friend in Gallatin, Tennessee, for years, but she had been a little girl, someone to tease and play with. Now on a visit to Gallatin, Sam found that Eliza was suddenly a young lady—eighteen years old and irresistible.

This time Sam knew that what he felt was true love, but it did not occur to him that true love might not be returned. Apparently he didn't consider that Eliza might think a thirty-five-year-old governor was a settled old man. From her point of view, Sam was her father's friend; why did he have to go sweet on her? But Eliza's family kept telling her what a good match this was. Sam kept telling her how much he loved her. Everyone agreed that she should say yes. Perhaps she hoped that she would feel different once they were married. In any case, she did give in.

Sam and Eliza were married on January 22, 1829, but after the wedding Eliza didn't feel one bit different. Even after weeks her feelings didn't warm up. Then one day, after three months of marriage, Sam came home from a trip earlier than he'd expected. If he had hoped for a nice wifely welcome, he was disappointed. Instead he found Eliza in tears and he lost his temper. No one knows what went on between them or what Sam said, but whatever he said, he was sorry he had said it. He took it all back and wrote a letter to Eliza's father. Eliza had been "cold" to him, he explained, but that did not excuse his words. He apologized and hoped everyone would go on as if this disagreeable incident had never occurred.

But it was too late. Eliza went back to her family and as

the news spread, rumors started. Sam's friends begged him to come out with the true story, whatever it was, for every day the rumors were growing more ugly and Sam was getting all the blame. But Sam wouldn't even tell his friends what had happened. He would not speak against a lady, he said. Nor would he ever talk of it again. He went into his room and locked the door. How could he continue as governor with people saying he had treated Eliza so badly? Yet how could he be a gentleman and clear his name? There was only one thing to do, he concluded. He'd have to quit as governor and leave Tennessee. He was feeling so depressed that before he left he decided to go to the Presbyterian minister who had performed the marriage ceremony and ask to be baptized. Although he had gone to church as a boy, he hadn't paid much attention to religion since. But perhaps if he were baptized, he would feel enough strength to go on with life, and heaven knew, he needed strength. When he asked for baptism, however, the minister turned him down. There were too many bad reports about him, the minister explained; he couldn't in good faith recommend him to the Lord. Sam walked out of the church. If this was church Christianity, he wanted none of it. If this was civilization, he was through. He'd go west and become an Indian again.

Chief Jolly and his people were now in Arkansas Territory, and as Sam proceeded—sometimes by foot, sometimes by riverboat—he dropped the Houston name and called himself Samuels. He was determined to put the past behind him, but he found it hard. He'd tasted success and been stung by ambition, yet here he was diving headlong into obscurity. Once he was so downhearted that as he leaned over the railing of a riverboat, he decided that his life wasn't worth living. He was about to leap into the water and end it all, but at that very moment an eagle swooped near his head, then with a wild scream soared into the sky, heading, as Sam said, "into the sunset." An eagle was Sam's medicine animal; it would only appear in this way if it had a special message. "I knew then," Sam wrote later, "that a great destiny waited for me in the west."

Even then Sam probably suspected that the eagle had Texas in mind. For who wouldn't want to play a part in the drama that surely lay ahead there? Land-hungry, enterprising American settlers were calling Texas the land of promise. Statesmen were building dreams around it. John Quincy Adams had tried to buy Texas from Mexico; Andrew Jackson also tried. But Texas was not for sale.

At the moment, however, Sam Houston had no clear idea of anything but that he must forget. He and John, a traveling companion, shared a poor opinion of civilization, and they decided one night not only to renounce civilization but to renounce it with style. And what, they asked, was more civilized than the clothes they wore on their backs? They'd get rid of them. So they built a bonfire and when the flames caught, Sam tossed in his hat. John did the same. In went his hat. (Then they both had a drink.) In went their coats. (Another drink.) Then their trousers, shoes, socks. All went into the fire until the two men stood stark naked, still drinking, watching civilization go up in smoke.

Luckily they each had another set of clothes to put on in the morning. But in any case when Sam reached the Cherokees, he began dressing as an Indian again in a white doeskin shirt with beads, yellow leather leggings, with a bright blanket around his shoulders. Indeed, now that he was back with Chief Jolly, Sam couldn't become Indian enough. As The Raven, his hair in a queue, he began making rash promises: he would never cut his beard; he would never speak English unless he absolutely had to; he would solve all the problems of the Cherokees. He would even bring Indians together in one great federation of the West.

Although he didn't make good on all his promises, he did

work hard at solving the Cherokees' problems and bringing peace to the Indians. Indeed, he forced himself into a frenzy of activity, traveling over the West, visiting tribe after tribe, proposing treaties. Sometimes he was successful and sometimes not, for the dissension was not only between tribes but within tribes unable to agree among themselves. Still, because of his efforts, the Osages, Creeks, and Cherokees managed to reach an agreement for the first time in thirty years. Actually, Sam Houston's lifelong record with the Indians was impressive: he signed more treaties with more tribes than any American agent or War Department official or president of the United States.

Yet the tireless, obsessive way he was now attempting to whip up cooperation among the Indians aroused suspicion in the United States. What was Sam Houston up to? How much was he aiding the Indians and how much was he promoting himself? There were all kinds of rumors: he was trying to build an empire in the West with himself as its head; he was planning to invade Texas with an army of Cherokees; he meant to conquer Mexico. Sam had a way of inspiring rumors—not always because of what he did but because he would never reveal his plans or explain his motives. He just went ahead on his own and acted. Also he was drinking more and more these days. It would have been easy to slip into loose talk that made him feel big but didn't mean much. Probably Sam himself had no clear idea of what would come out of his frantic activity, but certainly he hoped to benefit along with the Indians and the country itself. When Andrew Jackson wrote Sam a worried letter about the reports he'd been hearing, Sam reassured him. He would never do anything against his country, he replied. He might long for glory, but he would never willfully let Jackson down.

Still, he drove himself so hard over the summer of 1829

that by the time he returned to Chief Jolly's, he was sick not only from exhaustion but with malaria. Chief Jolly put Sam to bed on a mattress of cornstalks and called the medicine man. In the Cherokee world, fevers were thought to be caused by insects and worms taking revenge on people for stepping on them. In order to overcome the fever, the medicine man would fill his mouth with a magic solution of tobacco juice cooked over seven coals. Then at sunrise on four successive days he would blow this juice over four parts of the patient's body. It may have taken more than four days for the magic to cure Sam, but when he did recover, the Cherokees considered him one of their own. In an official ceremony they adopted him into the tribe.

Sam was as Indian now as he could get, but he went one step farther. He married Chief Jolly's lovely niece, Tiana. Of course the marriage would not be recognized in the civilized world, since he already had a wife. But what was civilization to Sam? And what was Eliza? The very thought that anyone might feel sorry for him on account of Eliza was "as cold," he said, "as the breezes of Norway." Yet Sam carried Eliza's engagement ring in a little buckskin bag around his neck. And whenever he saw a newspaper, his old ambitions flared. "It is hard for an Old Trooper," he wrote Andrew Jackson, "to forget the *Note* of the *Bugle*."

He was torn by conflicts, and the best way to forget, he discovered, was to blot everything out by drinking. He worked hard for the Cherokees, writing articles on their behalf in the *Arkansas Gazette*, helping them get rid of corrupt agents, but when he ran for a seat on the Cherokee Council, he was defeated. Depressed, seeing no future for himself in any world, he made a wild trip to Tennessee to try to get back in politics. But no one took him seriously. Before returning to Arkansas, he went to an artist in Nashville and paid for a full-length portrait of himself posing as

Caius Marius in exile. Exchanging his Indian clothes for a makeshift toga, standing in his bare feet, he asked the artist to paint in a background of crumbling columns. It was a dramatic gesture, as if he were telling the world, "I'll show you." Like Marius, he would be back. But right now he was depending so much on liquor that the Cherokees were calling him "The Big Drunk."

The death of his mother in the fall of 1831, however, had a sobering effect on him. Receiving word from Tennessee that she was sick, he rushed to her bedside. All his life Sam said that there was no love in the world as strong as the love of a mother for her children and surely on this last visit, his mother made Sam feel the strength of her love. Somehow she must also have reached the young man deep inside him, the young man who had put on her ring and marched off to fight the Creeks. And Sam must have promised himself (and perhaps her) that he'd make good again. Somehow. Sometime.

But a few months later (in December 1831), when Sam went with a delegation of Cherokees to Washington, he had no idea that this might be the time. As far as he was concerned, he was only making a visit as he had done before with his Indian friends. Perhaps he stayed longer than he expected. As it turned out, he stayed long enough to get into the middle of a spectacular fight that put him back in the limelight where he was at his best.

In a formal session of Congress Representative William Stanbery of Ohio, one of Jackson's most outspoken enemies, accused Houston of being part of a crooked scheme to obtain a contract for Indian rations. Enraged, Sam Houston decided immediately to take the knighthood route, but when he sent Stanbery his note of challenge, Stanbery did not reply. Instead he began carrying a pair of pistols as if he expected Sam to shoot him down in cold blood. Sam had no desire to kill the man if he couldn't do it in an honorable way, but

he didn't want him to go free either. And on the night of April 13, while walking back to his hotel with two friends, Sam saw his chance.

William Stanbery happened to be on the other side of the street. Sam crossed over.

"Are you Mr. Stanbery?" he asked.

"Yes, sir," Stanbery replied.

"Then you are a damned rascal." Sam raised the cane he was carrying and brought it down on Stanbery's head. When Stanbery turned to run away, Sam jumped on his back and threw him down. But Stanbery had his pistols and in the scuffle he pulled one out, held it against Sam's side, and pulled the trigger.

Luckily, Sam's Destiny was on the job. The gun did not go off and Sam was able to grab the pistol from Stanbery's hand. Then Sam lifted Stanbery's feet up as he lay on the ground and gave him a sound thrashing on his bottom as if he were a schoolboy.

Washington exploded when it heard the news. Stanbery persuaded the House of Representatives to arrest Sam and try him in the House itself. For one month the trial went on while the town buzzed with talk: How did the case go today?

The first day did not go well for Sam. Francis Scott Key was the lawyer defending Sam, and although one would think that a man who could write "The Star-Spangled Banner" would be a master of words, he made such a poor impression that Andrew Jackson was worried. Since all of Jackson's enemies were lined up solidly with Stanbery, Jackson was anxious for Sam to win for both their sakes.

He called Sam into his office and looked him over. Sam was still in his Indian clothes. Although Jackson had once thanked God that Houston was one man "made by the Almighty and not by a tailor," at the moment a tailor seemed to be in order. "Are those the only clothes you have?" Jackson asked.

When Sam admitted that they were, Jackson handed him a purse full of money and told him to buy some clothes suitable for his trial. And see what he could do, Jackson added, to put some fire in the defense.

Sam described the new outfit he bought: "a coat of the finest material reaching to my knees, trousers in harmony of color and latest style ... with a white satin vest to match."

As for his defense, Francis Scott Key took sick in the middle of the trial and rather than replace him, Sam took over himself. He was in his element now—the center of the show, back on the floor of the House of Representatives, of which he had once been a member, talking as he had never talked before, leaving out nothing. Freedom and patriotism—they had a bearing on his case; Shakespeare had words that applied; Greece and Rome—even they came to his defense. If he had been Caius Marius, he could not have done better. At the conclusion of his last speech, he was cheered. Still, when it came to a vote, the Speaker of the House was directed to reprimand Sam, but it turned out to be such a mild reprimand, there was no cause for shame.

"I do reprimand you accordingly," the Speaker said in the same matter-of-fact tone that he'd use to adjourn a meeting.

Sam was back in the civilized world. Visiting the Jacksons after the trial, Sam took Eliza's ring out of its buckskin bag and gave it to Sarah Jackson, the wife of Jackson's adopted son, Andrew, Jr. For the next few months while Sam was still in Washington, he spent most of his time at the White House with Jackson, reestablishing their old partnership.

"I was dying out," he said later, "and had they taken me before a justice of the peace and fined me ten dollars, it would have killed me. But they gave me a national tribunal for a theatre, and that set me up again."

There was no question about where Sam would go now.

Texas, of course. During his trial he had already been writing letters about the purchase of land, for he intended to become a citizen. The time was ripe. Mexico, worried about how many Americans had settled in Texas, had for a time closed Texas to immigration, but recently new Mexican leaders had opened it up again. But there were taxes, restrictions, arrests, and the white settlers (20,000 of them) were about to petition to become a separate Mexican state. Some even went farther. Why not a separate republic? Sam had no trouble visualizing a separate republic. He could even picture himself as president.

In November of 1832 on a final visit to Cherokee country, Sam said good-bye to Tiana and gave her his house, his land, and two slaves. Then, mounted on horseback, Sam, thirty-nine years old now, set off for his new life. As he crossed the Red River into Texas, an eagle circled over him. He might almost have expected that eagle because clearly this was where Sam Houston belonged. "The finest country to its extent in the globe," he wrote Andrew Jackson.

CHAPTER **3**

One of the first things Sam did was to travel across 500 miles of Texas, meeting people, getting the lay of the land so he could report to Andrew Jackson. This first report was full of enthusiasm, of optimism; how could it be otherwise? The very size of the country was exciting to a man who thrived on bigness. Indeed, if Jackson was interested in Texas, Sam said, this would be a good time to acquire it.

Of course Jackson was interested. But he was having too much trouble with the states that were already in the Union to risk a war by reaching out for a new one. At the moment South Carolina was the troublemaker. Because Jackson had imposed a tariff that, according to the South, favored the North, John C. Calhoun of South Carolina introduced what was called the doctrine of nullification. No state, he declared, had to obey an act by the national government if it didn't approve of it. Moreover, if the national government tried to use force, that state had a right to secede from the Union.

Calhoun might as well have waved a red flag under the nose of Andrew Jackson. Secession! The very word threatened everything that Jackson had built his life on.

"To say that any state may at pleasure secede from the Union," Jackson declared, "is to say that the United States is not a nation."

Informally he made himself even more clear. "If one drop of blood be shed...in defiance of the laws of the United States," he warned, "I will hang the first man of them I can get my hands on to the first tree I can find."

Only after Jackson had modified the tariff act did Calhoun stop his nullification talk. But division in the country remained and would become more acute as the country expanded. Slavery was behind it. If new territory were admitted to the Union, the question was, would it be free territory, adding to the power of the North, or would it be slave territory, adding to the power of the South? Under no circumstances did Andrew Jackson want to encourage the rival feeling of one part of the nation over another. Much as he might long for expansion, the Union was all important to him.

Sam Houston congratulated Jackson for his strong stand against nullification. And when Sam became actively involved in Texas politics, he understood that Texas would have to stand alone. There would be no official help from the United States, at least not for a while.

It didn't take Sam long to get involved. Settling in Nacogdoches in the eastern part of Texas, he set up a law practice, became a Mexican citizen, joined the Catholic church (required by Mexican law of all citizens), and added the name of a saint to his own name (also required). He chose Saint Paul and signed his name Paul Sam Houston. And of course he bought new clothes for himself (fancy embroidered ponchos) and new gear for his horse (a decorated saddle with silver plates and buckles). According to one admirer who saw him on horseback, he was "one of the most magnificent specimens of physical manhood."

Among his many new friends were Colonel Henry Raguet

and his seventeen-year-old daughter, Miss Anna. She was a pretty young lady with a special talent. Apparently she could flirt with Sam and teach him Spanish at the same time. They played a kind of game of courtship as if he were a knight and she were his lady fair. Sam may have taken the game more seriously than she did, but the important thing to Sam right now was Texas. What was going to happen to Texas?

Although Texans were divided as to whether they should try to work out their problems with Mexico peacefully or try to win a war of independence, there was at the moment some hope for peace. The former dictator of Mexico who had caused Texas so much trouble had just been defeated in a civil war by Santa Anna, a man who was thought to be sympathetic to democratic ideas. Now was the time for Texas to apply to Mexico for separate statehood with a constitution that would guarantee the kind of freedoms and security that settlers from the United States had learned to expect.

Although Sam Houston had been in Texas less than four months, he was elected in March 1833 to represent the district of Nacogdoches at a convention in April. It was not surprising that Sam should be recognized so soon and that he should be appointed chairman of the committee to write a constitution. After all, he'd been governor of a state and a United States congressman; who in Texas had more experience? And if the constitution turned out to be "one of the best" in existence as Sam claimed—what else would one expect? As it happened, the constitution was signed practically on the anniversary (just one day short of a year) of Sam's thrashing of Stanbery. This was significant, for as Sam figured it, that was the day that he had reentered civilization. As always, he was quick to read meaning into the fall of events.

The convention sent Stephen Austin (the man who had

brought the first American settlers into Texas) to Santa Anna with a petition for separate statehood and a copy of the proposed constitution. With Austin gone (much longer than anyone expected), Sam had time to size up his fellow Texans and make some prophecies.

Texans on the whole, he believed, tended to be rash and wild. All new states, he said, were "infested...by a class of noisy, second-rate men, who are always in favor of...extreme measures." But Texas was "absolutely overrun by such men." They were an independent bunch, not used to taking orders, not disposed to making compromises necessary for group action. Although Sam hoped for eventual independence, he worried that these daredevil extremists would rush into revolution without plan or preparation. As Sam saw it, he was the most steady man around.

As for his predictions (made in April 1834): within a year, he said, Texas would be a separate Mexican state; within three years it would be independent. Annexation would have to wait.

But Sam Houston was not always a good prophet. In the very month that he was making his predictions, Santa Anna did away with all state governments in Mexico and set himself up as a military dictator with absolute power. When Stephen Austin finally returned to Texas in September 1835, he announced that the next step was war. Austin had been imprisoned during part of his long enforced stay in Mexico and had nothing good to say about Santa Anna. Indeed, what could you expect from a man who declared that even if he could be made God, he'd still want something higher?

Already Santa Anna was sending troops over the border. San Antonio was occupied, and soldiers were ordered to disarm Texas and take all the cannon they could find. The first cannon they found was in the town of Gonzales, east of San Antonio. As soon as the Texans heard the Mexicans were coming, they gathered, one hundred strong, and hung a sign on their cannon. "Come and Take Me," the sign said. When the Mexicans didn't come, the Texans attacked and sent the Mexicans running.

This was encouraging; still it was obvious that Texas should get organized. In November a provisional or temporary government was established, and Sam Houston was appointed a major general in the army. War was in the air and as always in the beginning of a war, the talk was of glory. "Liberty and Texas—our wives and our sweethearts!" This was the toast whenever glasses were raised. From all over the United States, men—singly and in small groups—streamed into Texas to help with the fight. Sam put on his general's uniform, and in keeping with the courtly spirit, Miss Anna tied on the general's sword sash and cut off a lock of the general's hair to remember him by.

But if Sam felt like a hero, it was not for long. The provisional government was making a mess out of starting a war. It was doing nothing to supply Sam with army equipment and would not even give him power to appoint his officers. As a result, Sam found himself among rival officers with independent units, each going his own way. Moreover, if Sam gave an order, he could never be sure if the government would countermand it or if even his army, such as it was, would see fit to obey.

Sam had boasted that he was the most steady man around and indeed, in spite of all his difficulties, he seemed to be. He kept warning Texans not to be in a hurry. Wait for cannon to arrive. Drill the men. Over and over he repeated what he hoped would become the motto of the army: "Better do well late than never."

But Texans, as Sam had already pointed out, were not cautious, wait-around people. In December a small army of about 300 decided to take on that main force of Mexicans that held San Antonio. Five days the army fought—from street to street, house to house—and in the end over 1000

Mexicans surrendered, including their general who happened to be Santa Anna's brother-in-law. They were allowed to return to Mexico on the promise that they would never fight Texas again.

Of course Texas celebrated. The war was over! But Sam Houston was one of those who knew better. Santa Anna would never allow Texas to get away with this. The Mexicans would be back—probably in the spring, he figured. In the meantime Sam had the Texans themselves to deal with. They were causing such trouble that it was a wonder Sam could keep as "cool and sober" as he claimed to be doing. "Instead of eggnog," he wrote a friend, "I eat roasted eggs in my office."

The governing council was the worst offender. Every day it was taking over powers that were none of its business. When General Houston sent orders to Colonel Neill, in charge of San Antonio's stronghold, the Alamo, to remove the cannon and blow up the place, the council secretly told the defenders of the Alamo to do nothing of the sort. Houston knew that any group of men trying to defend the Alamo from within would be trapped, but the council believed otherwise. Acting as if they alone were in charge, the council members deposed the governor and in effect removed the army from Houston's command. The deposed governor, pretending that he still held power, gave Sam Houston a furlough until March 1 when the government was scheduled to meet and reorganize.

Sam went straight to Indian country in east Texas to make sure that the Cherokees and the twelve bands associated with them would support Texas in a war. He wasn't worried about the Cherokees' Chief Bowles (or "The Bowl," as he was called); he was one of Sam's closest friends and staunchest allies.

Meanwhile the defense of Texas lay in the hands of a Colonel Fannin and 430 men in the town of Goliad between

San Antonio and the coast. In San Antonio itself there were even fewer men—less than 200 who had, in spite of Sam Houston's warning, holed up in the Alamo. Later it was said that the men stayed because they couldn't find the oxen to move the fourteen cannon at the fort. More likely they stayed simply because they were high-spirited men who had traveled a distance just for the chance to fight tyranny. (Only seven were native Texans.) Closed up together behind the thick stone walls of the Alamo, they became a solid community of courage, their heroic feelings expanding under the pressure of cramped quarters. Moreover, they had three leaders whose very presence had a way of making men feel bigger than life. There was big, red-headed Jim Bowie, famous—among other things—for riding alligators bareback. And Davy Crockett, who boasted that he could lick his weight in wildcats and refused to believe that anything was impossible. In command (replacing Colonel Neill) was Buck Travis, who talked up death as if it were a glory. How could such men, closeted together, imagine that ordinary life still existed beyond these walls? How could they think that they were as mortal as other men? Let the Mexicans come, they said. Americans had beaten them once at San Antonio and they'd do it again.

On February 23 Santa Anna arrived with 1000 men. The first thing he did was to hang a bright red flag on top of a building within plain view of the Alamo defenders. There was no doubt what the message meant: *No mercy to men who don't surrender!* In answer, the Alamo defenders fired a cannon.

"I will never surrender or retreat," Colonel Travis wrote the next day in a letter asking for more men and more guns. The letter was addressed: "To the People of Texas & all Americans in the world," and it was signed: "Victory or Death."

Travis also sent Colonel Fannin a letter, but Fannin was

not a "Victory or Death" man. When at last he did see fit
to stir himself, his wagons broke down, his oxen balked,
and in the face of such reverses Fannin went no farther.

On February 29 Travis's letter reached the little town of
Washington-on-the-Brazos, where the March 1 convention
was to take place. It was not much of a town, little more
than a ferry crossing with a dozen makeshift cabins, all deep
in mud at the moment. The only building that had a wooden
floor was an unfinished shop owned by a gunsmith; it was
here that the delegates were gathering to keep out of the
rain. Sam Houston joined them that evening, his arrival
creating "more sensation," according to one observer, than
that of any other man.

There is no doubt that the situation in San Antonio in-
spired the men the next day to settle down to work without
the usual speechmaking. The first order of business was to
write a declaration of independence; otherwise what would
a victory against Mexico signify? Huddled around a table
in the gunsmith shop, the delegates worked in freezing tem-
peratures all day and far into the night. On March 2, 1836,
the declaration was signed. Sam wrote his name large as he
always did with the "S" looking more like a big "I," standing on its own. His signature looked as if he were saying,
"I am Houston," which would seem appropriate for a Man
of Destiny. Surely he never felt more like one. On that very
day, March 2, he became forty-three years old. That he and
Texas should celebrate the same birthday would have seemed
almost inevitable to Sam. More and more he was coming
to feel that he *was* Texas. And on March 4 when he was
elected commander in chief of the army, it was clear to him
that his future and the future of Texas were inseparable.

Up to this time the delegates had not been unduly alarmed
by the fate of the Alamo. Fannin was on his way, one del-
egate reported in his diary. "It is believed that the Alamo
is safe." But on March 6 the convention received a second

(and last) letter from Travis. The defenders of the Alamo were running out of ammunition. Fannin had not come. There were as many as 6000 Mexicans attacking them. The members of the convention wanted to break up the meeting and rush off then and there to San Antonio, but Sam said no. They should sit tight and get on with the business of forming a government. The reason they were all in such a mess now was that there had been no government.

Of course Sam didn't know as he rode off for San Antonio that it was already too late. That very day Santa Anna's army had breached the walls of the Alamo and entered.

"The Mexicans are upon us!" Travis had shouted. "Give 'em Hell!"

The defenders had fought as long as they had breath to fight, but in the end every man was killed. The Mexicans carried the bodies outside, piled them up, and set them on fire.

Less than three weeks later the Mexicans found Fannin and his men. Instead of fighting, Fannin's group surrendered immediately, expecting to be taken as prisoners. But this was not Santa Anna's way. Every man in arms was considered a traitor and so Fannin and his men were lined up and shot.

The independence of Texas was now up to one man— Sam Houston—and his army, which varied in number from week to week but which at its maximum in April was 1400. If Sam failed, Texas would fail. He could not afford to make a single mistake. So while he whipped up enthusiasm on one hand, he advised caution on the other. His strategy was to concentrate, retreat, and conquer. Draw the enemy inland. Don't use forts; fight in open country and in ravines. Wait until the time was right. Let the enemy make mistakes. "Better do well late than never." He said it again and again.

But Texans in and out of the army were wild to get back

at the Mexicans and had no use for such careful talk. Retreat was for cowards, they said. When you had a score to settle, you simply rolled up your sleeves, doubled up your fists, and let swing.

David Burnet, provisional president of the government, wrote to Houston: "The enemy are laughing you to scorn ... You must retreat no further."

But not all the men under Sam's command were always so eager to fight. As Santa Anna's troops advanced through Texas, burning down towns as they went, panic spread among citizens and infected the army. At one point Sam had two graves dug at the army campsite and posted notices on the trees. The first two deserters caught would be shot and buried there, the notices read.

On April 20 Sam had approximately 900 men with him as he made camp in a grove of live oak trees on a bluff that backed up to the San Jacinto River. He knew that Santa Anna and his army of about 1500 men had burned the temporary capital of Texas at Harrisburg (now part of Houston) and was marching in search of Sam's army. Hunkered down behind a rise of ground, partially hidden by a screen of Spanish moss, the Texas army watched the Mexicans approach across the plains. Each army knew where the other was, but the Mexicans may not have been aware that on each side of the grove of oak trees was a cannon. The Twin Sisters, the Texans called them—a gift from Cincinnati, Ohio. Beside the cannon were piles of broken horseshoes to be used as ammunition. When the Mexicans opened fire with their rifles, the Twin Sisters responded with their horseshoes.

So Santa Anna decided not to attack immediately. Instead he set up camp just where Sam wanted him to—between marshes and a boggy bayou. This was Santa Anna's first mistake. Sam had all the bridges across the river destroyed so that the only escape was through the marshes or down the road toward Harrisburg, which was controlled now by the Texans.

Sam's men could see that retreat was over. So why wait? Let them start now, they begged. Let them shoot it out once and for all.

But Sam said no. Not yet. He didn't explain. Whatever grumbling there was, he simply ignored. He was waiting for the Mexicans to make a second mistake. And by three o'clock on the afternoon of the next day (April 21), he figured that they had. Santa Anna, who had waited all day for something to happen, had decided that it was safe to take an afternoon nap. His army did the same.

Now, Sam said. At last. He gave three taps on a drum, the signal to call the troops together.

By four o'clock the Twin Sisters had been moved into firing position. Sam was on his white stallion, Saracen, and as the troops, arranged in battle order, advanced, the fife and drum corps struck up a tune. The only song they knew was a popular love song: "Will you Come to the Bower I Have Shaded for You?" It would have to do. In any case, they were soon drowned out by cries of "Remember the Alamo!" Then by rifle fire as the Mexicans and Texans met at point-blank range.

In the first round of fire a bullet shattered Sam's ankle and shot down Sam's horse. He grabbed another horse and when that too fell, he jumped on a third horse and, as his boot filled with blood, he continued to fight. It was all over in eighteen minutes. The Mexicans, taken by surprise, threw down their weapons and surrendered.

Texas was free.

The total loss to Texas was 6 killed, 25 wounded (including Sam), while the Mexicans had 630 killed, 208 wounded, and 730 taken as prisoners. Santa Anna was not among the prisoners, but Sam was not surprised. He'd show

up, Sam predicted, dressed "as a common soldier and on all fours," sneaking off somewhere.

That night the army celebrated, dancing around bonfires, whooping it up. Undoubtedly Sam, in spite of his painful wound (or perhaps because of it), joined in the drinking. But the two people he would most want to share this victory with were not with him—Miss Anna and Andrew Jackson.

The next day Sam wrote to Jackson, and as he lay under a tree while a doctor worked on his ankle, he braided some leaves to form a garland. He had been so busy being a general, he hadn't had time to play the part of a knight to his lady fair. He had always said he'd like to tilt in a tournament for her favor. Now he had tilted and as a trophy of his victory, he sent Miss Anna a garland accompanied by a note: "These are laurels I send you from the battlefield of San Jacinto. Thine. Houston."

That evening a last prisoner was delivered to Sam Houston. Dressed in a blue smock and red felt slippers, he might have gone unrecognized, but when the other Mexicans saw him, they cried out, "El Presidente!" Santa Anna had found the clothes in an abandoned house, but when he had tried to escape, he couldn't get through the mud.

Texans had pictured Santa Anna as a monster, but here he was just a man in silly clothes at their mercy. Most probably hoped to see Santa Anna shot then and there, but Sam Houston had other plans. He would keep Santa Anna as a hostage and thus force Mexico to recognize the independence of Texas. Of course there were those who criticized Sam, but that didn't change anything. You couldn't "bludgeon" Sam Houston, a Texan once observed, into being anything other than what he was.

Most people were hailing him as "The Hero of San Jacinto." All his life he accumulated names (some not complimentary), but this was the one he liked best to hear. The very sound of the name seemed like a prize he had longed for since boyhood and had at last earned. Yet no one had told him that dreams have a price. Or that they can change.

Sam Houston paid a price. Being a hero may have been a comfort, but it did not win over Miss Anna. Apparently tired of their courtship game, she did not even acknowledge receiving Sam's garland. She returned Sam's gifts and though they remained friends, the romance Sam had hoped for never developed. Nor did being a hero relieve Sam's suffering. By the time he reached proper medical attention in New Orleans, his leg had become infected. The same doctor who had removed the bullet from his Horseshoe Bend wound now removed twenty fragments of loose bone from his leg. For weeks Sam hovered near death, and as a result of San Jacinto he limped for the rest of his life and had recurrent bouts of pain. Still, he did recover sufficiently to be elected the first president of the Texas Republic.

In his inaugural address on October 22, 1836, he stated flatly that Destiny had brought him to this office (but of course he couldn't imagine anyone else having the job). Still, being a hero and president of a brand-new republic of 65,000 people might once have satisfied him, but no longer. His dreams had broadened. Sam Houston wanted the world to take Texas seriously as a respectable republic, one founded squarely on the same principles that Washington and Jefferson and in his turn Andrew Jackson had honored. He wanted to be proud of Texas. He wanted to show it off. So he dressed up in velvet, wore lace and a crimson vest, and he bragged of the new capital city that was being built. In the first three months of 1837, he reported, Houston City had grown from one log cabin to one hundred houses ("some of them fine frame buildings"). Fifteen hundred people lived there now and Sam added, "I have not seen a drunken man since my arrival." The town might still be ankle-deep in water and his own residence just a two-room log cabin, but already a ball had been given with seventy-three persons attending. "You have no conception of the reality," he wrote a friend. "It seems like magic."

Running a government, however, was not as easy as building a city. Actually, Sam did remarkably well in his term of office. He managed to get the justice system established, courts in session, salaries paid, mail delivered, and square pillars on the front of the capitol building. But always he faced obstruction. The legislature refused to ratify his treaty with the Cherokees, which guaranteed their boundaries; the army got out of hand; Mexico threatened the borders. And money. There was hardly enough money to keep the country going. Sam and the majority of Texans agreed that the only lasting solution was for the United States to annex Texas. Indeed, at the first anniversary of the declaration of independence a toast was proposed to annexation and everyone cheered. The people approved of annexation and were tickled by the wording of the toast: "Uncle Sam's big cornfield and his son Sam's cotton patch—may they soon be united in one big plantation!"

The following day (March 3, 1837) Andrew Jackson officially recognized the independence of Texas. It was the last act of his administration. Sam was pleased that Texas had the standing now of a sister republic, but it was no nearer annexation than it had ever been.

But perhaps Sam's greatest frustration came from the enemies within his own government. His vice president, Mirabeau B. Lamar, hated Sam. Ex-president Burnet called Sam a "half-Indian," and when Sam countered by calling Burnet a "hog thief," Burnet challenged Sam to a duel. Sam brushed it aside. He had a pile of challenges on his desk, but he paid no attention to any of them. He was much too busy trying to govern Texas.

Toward the end of his administration Sam wrote to Jackson: "No man living can so well appreciate the difficulties which have beset me as yourself ... You, General, have left monuments of Glory to your country ... But you had an organized Government, and men who were accustomed to civil rule while I had to command a Government from chaos, with men who had never been accustomed as a community to any rule, but their passions, nor to any government but their will. You had experience with mature wisdom. I lacked experience." Yet Sam wanted Andrew Jackson to know that he was loyal to the principles "which you inculcated upon me in my early life." They would remain with him "while life lasts."

CHAPTER 4

During the last six months of Sam's term of office, he was depressed. According to the constitution, a man was not allowed to be president twice in a row, so now, just when Texas was getting on its feet, Sam would have to turn over the presidency to someone else. Sam didn't object to the law. He was a strong believer in constitutions, but he had no use for the man who was probably going to take his place, Mirabeau B. Lamar. Lamar was against everything that Sam believed in. Against the Indians. (He called the Cherokees "Sam Houston's pet Indians.") And against annexation. Why reduce Texas to a mere state, he asked, when it was a glorious, growing country in its own right? Actually, Lamar was as enthusiastic as Sam was about Texas. Like Sam, he believed that Texas was God's chosen land, but he believed that Lamar, not Sam, was God's chosen leader of Texas. In Sam's opinion Mirabeau Lamar was nothing but an impractical dreamer, a highfalutin man who needed to be taken down a buttonhole or two.

All Sam could do was hope that Lamar would be defeated at the polls. There were two men running against him: Chief Justice Collingsworth of the Supreme Court and Peter A.

Grayson, an able and honest lawyer. But before the election Chief Justice Collingsworth jumped into Galveston Bay and drowned himself. Soon after, Peter Grayson in a sudden fit of dejection put a pistol to his head and blew his brains out. It certainly looked as if Destiny was at work, but Destiny was confused and working for the wrong man. Of course Sam was discouraged. If he spent too much time in his last months of office drinking, as his enemies claimed, it is not surprising, for steady as Sam was in many ways, drinking was still a weakness with him.

Sam was not drunk, however, on the day that Mirabeau Lamar was inaugurated president. Indeed, as it turned out, he was very much in charge not only of himself but of the whole show. He had not been invited to attend the ceremony, but when he stepped out on the porch of the capitol building, where the inauguration was to take place, it was clear that he intended to be the star. Sam Houston was in costume. Wearing a powdered white wig, buckled shoes, and knee-length pantaloons, he was dressed as George Washington. This was his way of saying that he was not only the Founding Father of Texas but that he was the man following in Washington's footsteps, the one who should be listened to.

The crowd went wild at the sight of Sam and, as he figured, called for him to speak. He was ready. Indeed, he had no notion of leaving the presidency without delivering a farewell speech. Sam spoke for three hours. And all the time there was Mirabeau B. Lamar sitting on stage, sweating, twitching, becoming more and more nervous, for, as Sam knew, Lamar was a fidgety man who could not bear to wait for anything. When Sam finally sat down amid enthusiastic cheers, Lamar was too upset to utter a word. He handed his inaugural address to his secretary and told him to read it to the crowd.

Once he was president, Lamar started to remake Texas.

One of the first things he wanted to do was to move the capital. Instead of having it in a city named for Sam Houston, he decided to start from scratch and build a new city in the center of the country. Once on a buffalo hunt he'd seen a beautiful spot surrounded by seven hills on the banks of the Colorado River. A perfect place for the capital, he thought. He'd call it Austin for Stephen Austin, the true father of Texas who had brought the first settlers to the country. This was a good name, not only because Austin had been well liked but because he was dead and couldn't disagree with Lamar or anyone else. (He had died in 1836.)

As far as Sam Houston was concerned, however, moving the capital to a position so close to both Mexico and the warlike Comanche Indian tribe was a crazy idea. But then, in Sam's opinion, Lamar had many such ideas. And when his ideas failed, what did Lamar do? Don't worry, he'd tell the people. Nothing could go seriously wrong in Texas as long as everyone was patriotic enough.

Sam didn't care to hang around and watch Lamar make his mistakes, so in the spring of 1839 he went to the Hermitage to visit Andrew Jackson. On his way back he stopped in Alabama at the plantation of William Bledsoe, who raised purebred horses. Sam was interested in buying horses and in selling Texas land, and when he heard that Mrs. Bledsoe was giving a strawberry festival, he was interested in that too. Sam Houston loved a party, and this one turned out to be the most important party he had ever attended. He was sitting in the rose garden with Mrs. Bledsoe when her twenty-year-old sister, Margaret Lea, walked up with a basket of strawberries on her arm. Tall and beautiful with unforgettable violet eyes, Margaret fell in love with forty-six-year-old Sam Houston on the spot. As for Sam, he knew that Margaret was the one whom Destiny had been saving for him all these years. There should be no obstacles. Sam's divorce from Eliza had been legalized the year before, Tiana was dead, so in every way he was free and ready to marry. When he left, Sam gave Margaret Lea a bouquet of garden pinks, which she pinned in her hair. If she did not actually say yes on this visit, she did a few months later when he returned.

But there were obstacles. Margaret's family was against the marriage. Sam Houston had a reputation as a heavy drinker, they pointed out. He didn't attend church and had not even been baptized. These were serious faults, especially for such a religious person as Margaret, but she was not daunted. She would reform him, she said. But he was too old for her! Margaret Lea remained serene through all the objections. Her answer was simple and final. "He has won my heart," she said. And that was that.

Margaret and Sam were to be married in May of the following year (1840). Meanwhile Margaret began making her trousseau: a white satin dress, a purple silk dress, and a blue muslin one. And Sam went back to Texas to check on what Lamar was up to.

What Sam found infuriated him. While he had been out of the country and unable to interfere, Lamar had fought and defeated the Cherokees. Sam knew of course that Lamar hated all Indians. The white man had shown nothing but kindness to Indians, Lamar claimed, but kindness didn't work. It was time to either drive them out of the country or kill them all. It made no difference that the Cherokees felt that they had a right to their land. The Mexicans had approved of the Cherokee settlement (though not in writing) and the Texans had made a boundary treaty with the Cherokees that Sam Houston still hoped would be formally signed. Right up to the end, Sam's good friend The Bowl, the tall, red-headed chief (son of a Scotch-Irish father and a Cherokee mother), had tried to avoid war. But the Texans' demands were too harsh and the young men in his tribe were too eager to fight. So, although he was eighty-three years old, this vigorous, dignified old man took up the sword that Sam Houston had given him and mounted his sorrel horse. He had foreseen that his people would be beaten, and when they were, he was the last man to leave the battlefield. Leading his wounded horse, he was walking away when he was shot in the back. He forced himself to sit up and face his enemies. The captain of the attacking Texas company shot The Bowl in the head.

When Sam heard the news, he delivered a scorching speech in which he said that The Bowl was a better man than any of his murderers. Then Sam took up residence in the new capital at Austin, which he described as "the most unfortunate site upon earth for the Seat of Government." From his little dirt-floored shanty Sam watched Lamar go his merry way, talking patriotism while he ran the country deeper and deeper into debt. His final and wildest scheme was to send an expensive expedition to take possession of the territory around Santa Fe, which Texans claimed was theirs but was still in Mexican hands. When the legislature did not approve the expedition, Lamar went ahead anyway. From the first the project was doomed, and as any practical man might have guessed, all 321 men in the expedition were captured by the Mexicans.

"I might have been happy in ignorance at home," Sam Houston remarked, "had I known the full extent of Lamar's stupidity."

By this time Sam and Margaret were married and had settled in the summer home Sam had bought at Cedar Point on Galveston Bay. Some of Sam's friends had predicted that the marriage wouldn't last six months. His temperament was not suited to family life, they said; he would never be happy. But Sam fooled his friends. He was extremely happy, and though it took some time for Margaret to interest her husband in church, she was able to get him to swear off drink right away. Of course it was hard. For a while Sam carried a little vial of ammonia with him to sniff when he felt the urge to drink. When he was away from home, he wrote Margaret not to worry. He had gone on no "sprees." They did not even keep liquor in the house, and when Sam Houston was reelected president in September 1841, the celebration had plenty of "goodies in general," but, as one guest reported, it was "cold water doin's."

Sam was glad to be back in office, but Texas was in worse shape, he said, than it had been before San Jacinto. He couldn't even figure out how far in debt the country was, but he did know that there was not enough money in the treasury to buy firewood for the president's house. Besides, the house itself was in such a mess, it was hardly worth heating. When Lamar left, he hadn't put padlocks on the doors and looters had apparently gotten in. Mirrors, beds, mattresses, spoons, dinner plates were among the many items that Sam listed as being in such poor shape as to be practically unusable. Indeed, only a few things seemed to have survived unharmed: a couple of pitchers, a ruler, two paperweights. Not much use in housekeeping.

Sam put the government on a strict economy program, cutting his own salary in half and reducing the payroll from $174,000 a year to $32,800. But money wasn't the worst problem. Lamar's disastrous Santa Fe expedition had infuriated Santa Anna (now back in power in Mexico). Texans were mad too. They had heard that those 321 Texas prisoners had been tortured on their way to Mexico City. So it looked like war, but Sam knew that there was not enough money in Texas to win a war, especially if the Texans took the war into Mexico, which many were eager to do. On the one hand, Sam had to hold back the hotheads; on the other hand, he had to defend the country. He managed to get an army together, and fortunately the Mexicans retreated. At least for a while. All through 1842 they kept coming back, making raids, retreating, coming back again. The only permanent solution was annexation to the United States, but since Congress was still against it, Sam would have to figure out a way to change their minds.

Meanwhile, for safety's sake, he sent Margaret east to Liberty County, where her mother had moved. And he moved the capital from Austin back to Houston City. The people of Austin, however, were so unhappy about this that in the fall of 1842 Sam agreed to a compromise and moved the capital to Washington-on-the-Brazos. He tried to have the archives or state papers also moved to Washington, where they would be safe, but the people in Austin absolutely refused. Once the papers were gone, how could they be sure that they'd get the capital back to Austin again? The first time Sam sent for the papers, the people buried them. The next time, they waylaid the messenger, captured his horse, and shaved the horse's tail and mane. In the end they actually fought over the papers, and the people of Austin won what came to be known as the Archive War. Sam washed his hands of the whole affair. They'd just have to get along in Washington-on-the-Brazos without the historical records.

Washington itself had grown somewhat over the years, but as a capital city—even a temporary one—it was, Sam admitted, a joke. The war and marine department was housed in a log cabin that had only one window. The senate met on the second floor of a grocery store that specialized in selling liquor. The house of representatives was assigned a room over a saloon, and legislators were in the habit of stopping off at the bar. Many never made it up the stairs, so Sam had steps built on the outside of the building.

Indeed, Sam himself found it hard to stick to his cold-water program in the atmosphere of the present capital. In January 1843, he went to visit Margaret, who was expecting their first child in the spring, and he asked her to return with him to Washington-on-the-Brazos. He had gone "off the wagon," he confessed, and he needed Margaret to keep him sober. Margaret would have gone no matter where she had to live, but Sam made sure that she had the best quarters that Washington had to offer. He even had her rosewood piano hauled to Washington from Houston City and ordered new white chinaware, two wash pitchers, and upholstery material. The pattern should be of vines or flowers, he wrote. No "Turkey Gobblers, Peacocks...wild Boars, or Stud Horses!!!" (Sam loved exclamation points.) But if Margaret served tea in the afternoon from her silver tea service, Sam, for all his love of show, never put on airs. Like every other man in Washington, he shaved on the back porch near the pump every morning. He was fifty years old now, and perhaps because his hair was thinning, he took pride in the sideburns he'd begun to wear. He shaved around them carefully, even though he shaved army-style without a mirror and shaved before an audience. Politicians had discovered that the time to corner Sam for a talk was on his back porch in the morning.

The year 1843 was an improvement over 1842. Money was more stable, treaties of friendship had been signed with some of the Indian tribes, Mexico had not bothered Texas recently. "When have we seen crops gathered before, without fear of interruption?" Sam asked. But from Margaret and Sam's point of view perhaps the best thing that happened in 1843 was that Sam, Jr., was born on May 25. He was a stout fellow, Sam wrote. "May he not be a loafer or an agitator."

But all the time Sam, himself, was still struggling with the same problem that had been uppermost in his mind since 1836. How was he going to get Texas annexed to the United States? He pondered annexation as he whittled away on a piece of soft pine. He had a handsome new pocketknife from New Orleans and as always, whittling seemed to clear his mind. It would do no good simply to press for annexation, he decided. Twice Congress had voted it down. Texas would come into the Union as another slave state and of course the North was dead set against that. No, Sam figured, he'd have to find a roundabout way to get agreement. He wouldn't beg.

Instead Sam began to seek an alliance with England and France, one that would guarantee peace between Texas and Mexico. In return, England asked that Texas give up slavery. As anyone could see, such an alliance could in the future give England back that toehold on the continent that it had always wanted. It could be the beginning of a powerful new republic. The United States would be the loser if it didn't annex, Sam said. It didn't matter to Texas one way or the other.

Sam didn't explain what he was really up to, so of course no one understood. Did Sam want annexation or didn't he? Some people, including Andrew Jackson, worried. Jackson, in poor health and in retirement at the Hermitage, still wielded considerable political power, and he was determined that Texas should not go astray. He wanted it annexed before he died. When his favorite candidate for the 1844 presidential election (Martin Van Buren) came out against annexation, Jackson switched his support to James Polk, who won by a narrow margin.

In the midst of all this maneuvering, Sam Houston's term of office expired. In December 1844, he turned the presidency over to his friend Anson Jones and returned with his family to Liberty County. But like Jackson, Sam Houston was almost as powerful out of office as he had been in office. And in February 1845 he was so anxious about annexation that he told a friend that if the Congress of the United States had not passed an appropriate measure by March 4, he'd come out strong and work against it.

But on March 1 (three days before Polk was inaugurated) outgoing President Tyler, with Polk and Jackson both badgering him, finally signed an annexation resolution.

It was up to Texas now to agree to the terms. Still, no one was sure what Houston was going to do—not even Jackson, and he couldn't wait much longer. So he wrote Sam, and only then did Sam relent. Yes, he assured Jackson, Texas would agree. Furthermore, he and Margaret and young Sam were coming to the Hermitage for a visit and he would explain his actions.

Jackson received the letter on June 6. He felt better. "All is safe at last," he said.

On June 8 the Houstons arrived, but they were too late. Andrew Jackson had died just three hours before.

Personally grieved by the loss of his dear friend, Sam Houston must also have felt the hand of Destiny again. The timing of his arrival could not have been an accident. It was as if he was *meant* to carry on where Jackson had left off. Always committed to Jackson's principles, surely Sam felt a recommitment now. Again and again he would link himself with Jackson. "You know," he would say, "I am a Unionfier as General Jackson was."

CHAPTER 5

Although Texas legally became a state in December 1845, the official ceremony took place two months later in Austin, which had become the capital again. President Anson Jones lowered the Lone Star flag from the capitol building, and Sam Houston, standing at the foot of the flagpole, gathered it in his arms. No eagles circled in the skies, but Sam no longer needed eagles to confirm a historic moment.

Just as this was the end of one era for Texas, Margaret hoped that this would also be the end of Sam's public life. Sam certainly talked as if it would be. All he cared about now, he said, was domestic happiness. He began drawing plans for a new home fourteen miles from Huntsville; Raven Hill he would call it. Margaret was so happy that she wrote a ten-verse poem called "To My Husband."

> *Thy task is done. The holy shade*
> *of calm retirement waits thee now.*

She should have known better. Sam was forever talking retirement and peace. "I am a home man," he said, but he was too restless, too ambitious, too committed to resist the pull of politics. When Sam was elected a U.S. senator from the new state of Texas, he didn't hesitate—in a flash he was off for Washington, D.C. He was fifty-three years old now with a "lion-like" countenance, an observer said. And as usual, people remarked on his clothes. Often he would make his first appearance in a city wearing a Mexican blanket and a wide sombrero. It was as if he wanted to serve notice that he had his own way of doing things. Then, after he'd made his point, he'd go back to store clothes. In the Senate, which was filled with grave-looking men with long coats, dangling watch fobs, and eyeglasses that hung from black ribbons, Sam generally wore "a military cap and a short military cloak of fine blue broadcloth, with a blood-red lining."

In other words, he was noticed. He was impressive. Moreover, in spite of all his "home" talk, he had ambitions for the future and they must have shown. President Polk wrote in his diary that Sam had his eye on the presidency. One of Sam's Texas friends said that if Sam kept on as he was doing, he would "rent the White House." A Huntsville newspaper predicted that Sam would be president within ten years. Sam didn't talk, but he obviously hoped. He must have had the presidency in mind when he hired a man to write his biography. It was a truthful biography, the author insisted, but it was also a glowing one. "Were I the nation's ruler," Sam once wrote to Margaret, "I could rule it well."

But ruling the country was no simple matter. Hardly had Sam settled down in Washington when war was declared between the United States and Mexico. Mexico was angry that the United States had annexed Texas, but when it came to actual war, people still argue about which side started it. At the time Americans argued if there should even be a war, but Sam thought it was inevitable. The boundary between the two countries would never be settled without a fight, but he wasn't interested in fighting himself. After all, he had commanded an army and had no desire to serve under anyone else, particularly under a commander (General Winfield Scott) who was known in the army as "Old Fuss and Feathers." From Sam's point of view, the war was worth it. It went on for two years, but in the end the United States won and with it territory that stretched all the way to the Pacific Ocean.

Here was the coast-to-coast nation that Jackson and Houston had dreamed of, but unfortunately the dream was in danger. The question was, would the United States remain united or not? With every piece of added territory, the country renewed its argument over slavery. Should the new territory be slave territory or free territory? Sam Houston owned slaves but admitted that slavery should eventually be abolished, but in a peaceful way. Meanwhile, he refused to discuss whether slavery was right or wrong, legal or illegal. That was a question for the Supreme Court to decide, he said. Sam blamed hotheaded fanatics in both the North and the South for arousing the people to a pitch of feeling that might, if the country wasn't careful, burst into war.

Sam was particularly angry when John C. Calhoun called for a convention of Southern states so that the South could show its strength. Calhoun was up to his old tricks, Sam claimed. Trying to break up the Union just as he'd tried in Jackson's administration. This time Calhoun had a partner in his scheme—Jefferson Davis of Mississippi, whom Sam described as "cold as a lizard and as ambitious as Lucifer." Sam refused to have anything to do with Calhoun's movement, and when Southern radicals called him a traitor, Sam didn't even bother to defend himself. He had Jackson's words to back him up, and he used them again and again: "The Federal Union—it must be preserved."

But in 1850 Henry Clay introduced in the Senate a compromise bill that was supposed to end the controversy. The bill made provisions for the North to have its way on some matters and the South to have its way on others. Sam Houston hated words like "compromise" and "temporize." Since he didn't ever expect to "temporize" (give in to public opinion), he had crossed out the word in his dictionary and made a note in the margin, "Out with this!" He preferred "adjust" to "compromise," but whatever the bill was known by, he did approve of it. Indeed, he spoke in favor of the bill long and fervently, ending with words that Abraham Lincoln would later make famous: "A nation divided against itself," Sam said, "cannot stand." The bill passed.

Sam had been in Washington four years now, and at first Margaret had worried about what life in the capital city would do to him. "I fear," she had written, "lest they should steal your heart from God. There is something so bewitching in the voice of fame." But Margaret's influence remained strong. Sam spoke at meetings of temperance societies, admitting that though some people could drink moderately without bad effects, he could not drink at all. And he didn't. Perhaps to quiet Margaret's fears, he began attending church regularly. He sat in a front pew, whittling as he listened to the sermon. At the end of the service he gave the objects he'd whittled—crosses, hearts, hatchets—to children in the congregation. In the afternoon he wrote Margaret, telling her what the preacher had said. But when it came to joining the church, he couldn't bring himself to do it. He was afraid he didn't *feel* enough for baptism, he explained. He couldn't take the step unless he did it with a whole heart.

While he was away, Sam wrote faithfully to his family, which included three little girls now. (Eventually there would be eight children.) He was particularly concerned about the education of Sam, Jr., so he wrote long serious letters to his son, filled with advice about behavior. "Learn to be good when you are young," he wrote. "When you say your prayers, be grateful to God." "Boys should always be kind and generous to their sisters." Generally he ended his letters by telling Sam to "Say howdy to the servants." He also sent Sam presents: a picture of a lifeboat, an Indian rubber ball (a new invention that would never wear out, Sam said, if it didn't get too hot), a bedstead for young Sam's tent, and he bought six canaries but he wasn't sure how he was going to get them home.

Sam returned to Texas for those long stretches of time each year when Congress was not in session. When he went in 1850, it was not to Raven Hill but to a fairly new home in Huntsville, which he called a "bang-up place." Built like his boyhood home in Virginia, it had a long hall (called a dogtrot) running through the middle of the house, with doors at each end. When both doors were open, the family dogs could tear through the house—in one door and out the other—and if there was a breeze around, it could do the same thing. Sam had a separate log cabin on the grounds, which he used as a study. He could let the shavings from his whittling pile up on the floor without anyone interfering. Whenever he wished, he could spit into his spittoon and if he missed, it didn't matter. As a young man, he'd been criticized by ladies for spitting on their front porches instead of going to the railing to spit over the side. Presumably Margaret had cured him of this habit, but he did love that little study of his where nobody had to cure him of a thing.

Perhaps he'd just stay in Huntsville. He was so pleased that the Texas legislature had approved Henry Clay's compromise bill that he said, "I may now retire." He felt the Union was safe. Of course privately he thought it would be even safer if he were at the head of it, and everyone knew that no matter how he talked, he had no notion of retiring. People were already thinking of the presidential election of 1852.

Sam was thinking too. Indeed, this was the election that he had his heart set on and he had every reason to be encouraged. "Houston Clubs" were springing up here and there, and he kept busy speaking to crowds all over the country. He did not openly campaign for the presidency; only to friends did he confide his hopes. "Others have had their day," he wrote to one friend, "and mine is to come!" Yet it was obvious that he wanted to be president. An editor of the *New York Times* wrote that Sam would "do anything" to get the presidency. Thomas Rusk, the other senator from Texas, worried about Sam. "I think it will nearly kill him," he said, "if he fails."

Both men were wrong. Even for an office that he wanted desperately Sam Houston would not "do anything." Indeed, at the convention to nominate a candidate for the Democratic party, Sam voluntarily stepped out of the race. Seeing that there were so many candidates and the delegates could not agree on any one of them, he withdrew his name in order to support little-known Franklin Pierce, who seemed to have the fewest number of enemies. (Pierce won on the forty-ninth ballot.) Of course Sam must have been disappointed, but he didn't let on. He wrote home: "I would rather my children say ... 'My Father was a wise man and a patriot' than that he was President of the United States."

Still, Sam may have hoped that he'd have another chance four years later. As time went on, Sam doubted if Franklin Pierce would be reelected, since (in Sam's view) he was such a weak president. "He is a poor, a very poor dog skin," Sam wrote. Meanwhile Sam kept busy in Washington, making friends, trying to influence the government. Even when he was sick, he continued to work. Once a young New York lawyer called on him at his hotel and found him in bed with chairs lined up from his bed to the door. As one visitor left, the rest all moved up a chair.

But during the second year of Pierce's term of office (1854), the slavery issue boiled up again, and of course Sam jumped in to try and save the Union. Again it was new territory

that caused the trouble. Kansas and Nebraska were to be made official territories of the United States; should they be slave or free? Henry Clay, who had always tried to keep power equally balanced between the North and the South, had died two years before, and the spirit of compromise seemed to be gone. A Kansas-Nebraska bill was proposed, which would do away with all Clay's previous compromises and provide for the people in Kansas and Nebraska to decide for themselves whether they'd be a free territory or not.

Sam was enraged. He begged Congress to defeat the bill. Didn't they see what would happen? In their mad desire to win the vote, Northerners and Southerners would both rush to settle the territory. They'd do anything to gain more power for their side. The whole country would be stirred up—perhaps even to the point of bloodshed, perhaps eventually to civil war. He couldn't bear for his "beloved South" to go down in a "smoking ruin," Sam said, yet if it came to war, he was afraid that's what would happen. "Depend upon it," he warned, "if this bill passes, it will convulse the country from Maine to the Rio Grande."

Sam often made prophecies about the future, but he said he was like the ancient Greek prophetess Cassandra, who always told the truth but was never believed. In any case, the bill passed. Southerners thought they would profit by the bill and were furious with Sam for not sticking with the South. Texans who favored the bill accused Sam of being a traitor. The Texas legislature and the State Democratic Committee not only denounced him but told him that when his term as senator was over, he shouldn't look for public office again. Never had Sam been so viciously attacked, often with stories that were not true. Sometimes when Sam heard these stories, he just said, "Lie on!" Sometimes he became more eloquent. Once he remarked that he'd "let his enemies fester in the putrescence of their own malignity." He admitted that his stand on the Kansas-Nebraska bill was the most unpopular thing he'd ever done but also, he added, it was "the wisest and most patriotic." "Because the entire South is wrong," he once said, "should I be wrong too?" After all, the Union itself was at stake.

Sam was upset and worried. It was one of those times when whittling was not enough to clear his mind. Restlessness often overcame him and on the spur of the moment he would pack up his family and off they'd go to Cedar Point, to Houston, or to Independence, where Margaret's mother lived now. The year before Sam had built his own house in Independence, so he loaded the family in their big yellow coach drawn by four horses and set off for their new home. He had decided on the move not only because so many members of Margaret's family lived there but because Margaret suffered from asthma and he thought that she would do better among the hills of Independence. Moreover, Independence, known for its fine schools and for Baylor University, would be good for the children.

Every Sunday Sam went to the local Baptist church with his family. Sam was used to going to church and used to Margaret talking up baptism to him, but now Margaret had her mother and their good friend, the Reverend Mr. Burleson, to back her up. It was a powerful combination. Moreover, with all the political criticism being piled on him, Sam was in an emotional mood. He had named his newly born son (and sixth child) Andrew Jackson. The name itself would have been a comfort, for Sam must sometimes have felt that only he remembered Andrew Jackson and his principles. Only he in all the South was trying to preserve the Union. It would be nice to feel that God was on his side and that he was on the side of God. Then one Sunday morning at a revival service, Sam Houston's heart welled up and he knew that he was ready.

He was not the only one. The preacher must have used words that shook up souls, for there was a total of twenty people, including students from Baylor University, who also declared that they were ready. The baptismal service was to be performed on November 19 at the font, or special baptismal pool, behind the church where the twenty would be immersed.

This was big news in Independence—not only that so many were to be baptized but that Sam Houston was one of them. It was also a chance for mischief-minded boys to have some fun. The night before the ceremony a group of boys, possibly Baylor students, filled the font with rubbish. Of course it was unusable, but nothing was going to stop those twenty people from being saved, now that they had made up their minds. Rocky Creek was only a few miles away, so Reverend Mr. Burleson, the twenty converts, their friends, and many spectators trooped across the countryside.

While the spectators stood on the banks of Rocky Creek, Reverend Mr. Burleson, dressed in a white robe, waded into the waist-deep water. One by one, the twenty (also in white) stepped into the water. One by one, they were ducked under the surface and prayed over. When Sam's turn came, Margaret was so happy that, according to one Baylor student, she shouted like a Methodist. Margaret's mother, Nancy Lea, was so happy that she ordered a bell for the church. It weighed 502 pounds and was made of a combination of copper and tin, which, the foundry claimed, was "the most sonorous bell-metal known."

As for Sam, he took his baptism seriously but as usual he had a bit of humor to add to the occasion. When a friend remarked that he guessed Sam had all his sins washed away now, Sam replied that he hoped so. "But if they are all washed away," he said, "the Lord help those fish down below."

CHAPTER 6

Sam was sixty-three in March 1856 and he seemed to be surprised at the fact. "We were once young," he wrote a friend, "but are now old!!!" The three exclamation marks seemed to imply that he didn't expect anyone, least of all himself, to believe that he was *really* old. He might suffer from his San Jacinto wound and he might be lame, but he didn't feel old. "I am hardy as a bear," he insisted, "and young as ever."

Indeed he had to be strong because he was sure that the nation was going to need him. All his worst fears about Kansas and Nebraska were coming true. Southerners from Missouri had rushed into Kansas. Northerners from New England also. Each side had set up its own government and, just as Sam had predicted, there was bloodshed. One of the Northerners was a man named John Brown, who claimed to have direct instructions from God to set slaves free, no matter what he had to do. In Kansas he and six followers decided they had to kill five proslavery men. And they did. All the feelings of the North against the South and the South against the North were mounting to fever pitch. Even in

Congress there was violence. A senator from Massachusetts was beaten up by a congressman from South Carolina.

In August 1857, in the midst of all this turmoil, Hardin Runnels, a radical Southerner from Texas, announced his candidacy for governor of the state. Runnels was a secessionist, the same brand as Jefferson Davis was, and he declared that he was going to run an anti-Houston campaign. When Sam heard this, he hurried home. He was not going to let a secession-minded hothead take over his beloved state. At least not without a fight. He would run for governor too.

"The people want excitement," he said, "and I had as well give it as anyone." And indeed, who could match Sam Houston's flair for excitement? When he couldn't find a buggy to take him campaigning, he accepted an invitation to go with Ed Sharp, a plow salesman who was traveling around the country anyway. Riding in a crimson-colored buggy advertising "Warwick's Patent Plow" in enormous gilt letters, Sam attracted exactly the kind of attention that he wanted. To make sure that people turned out to hear him, he announced his arrival ahead of time in newspapers: "The Hero of San Jacinto is Communing with the People." Generally he had a crowd, and they laughed when they saw him jump down from that bright red buggy. No gold lace or fancy trimmings for Sam on this trip. He was a "man of the people," dressed in a plain linen duster that covered him from top to toe. On a hot day, if there were no women in the audience, he'd whip off the duster and the shirt beneath it and talk bare-chested. (The hair on his chest was thick as a mop, people said.) When there were women present, he toned down his style. Once when he spoke under a couple of oak trees, some ladies gave him a handmade flag. At the end of his speech, he made such a big show of kissing each one of those ladies that those two trees became known as the "Kissing Oaks." In sixty-seven days Sam Houston covered over 1550 buggy miles and delivered forty-seven blistering speeches. Sometimes he spoke for two hours, but when he really got into the swing, he'd go on for four hours without stopping.

At night he and Ed Sharp made camp outdoors. They had a coffeepot, a frying pan, and a gridiron, and when they had finished eating they spread their blankets on the ground and made themselves comfortable. No matter how much talking Sam had done during the day, he liked to end up with some old-time stories and a song or two.

Sam had warned his friends that he was going to hit Texas like a tornado and he did. He conducted an all-out, heroic campaign, but he did not win the election. It was the first time that Texas had turned him down. Still, Sam didn't waste time feeling sorry for himself.

"The fuss is over," he wrote, "and the sun yet shines... What next?"

Washington was next. He went back to fulfill the last two years of his senatorial term. He had been advised to resign, since his defeat in Texas would lessen his influence in the Senate, but he scoffed at the idea. Quit? Not Sam Houston. He still had a voice and a vote and he expected to use them to defend the Union. In case anyone thought he'd been made timid by his defeat, he wore a new catskin vest back to Washington. When he was asked whether the fur was from a wildcat (which it was), a panther, or a tiger, Sam replied that it was from none of these. It was a leopard skin, he said, and he wore it because, according to the Bible, a leopard cannot change his spots.

Sam used every opportunity to defend the Union, to promote justice for the Indians, and to rail against the military academy at West Point, which graduated men, he said, who couldn't even "track a turkey." He was fretful. He found fault with the Senate. It was not the respectful, dignified body that it used to be. Senators whispered now and rattled

around during speeches; they slouched in their seats and even put their feet on their desks. It was a disgrace.

Moreover, Sam couldn't stand the new statues in the Capitol. The Goddess of Liberty, for instance. She looked as if she were in such pain, Sam wondered if she had a boil under her arm. Or perhaps she was embarrassed by her shoes. Who ever heard of a Greek goddess in a pair of stout, hobnail-type shoes made for working in swamps? And what about the statue of the Indian squaw who didn't know how to hold her papoose? Straining its neck like a turtle, that poor little papoose was forced to hold up its head "stiff as an apple on a stick." Sam couldn't bear to think of it.

As time went on, Sam worried about Sam, Jr. After all, he was the oldest son and was expected to make his father proud. As a boy, Sam himself had never liked being told what to do, but he didn't hesitate to guide his son every step of the way. Sam, Jr., was seventeen years old and attending a military academy when his father scolded him for the sloppy way he folded his letters. He didn't think much of his son's handwriting either. He should "catch his pen far from the end," Sam said, and for practice he should copy his father's letters to the secretary of war and the secretary of the interior. And of course no son of Sam Houston's should go through life without having the example of Caius Marius to inspire him. So Sam mailed off a picture of his old hero and told young Sam to read Marius's story "at his first leisure."

Tired of life in Washington, Sam didn't even enjoy parties as he once had. He went to one for Harriet Beecher Stowe, the author of *Uncle Tom's Cabin*, but he found her "a hard subject to look on." He stayed an hour, ate some ice cream, and went home. All he wanted, he wrote Margaret, was to be with her and "let the world wag." He could not control the destiny of the country, he admitted, so he might as well retire to Cedar Point and raise sheep.

But Sam had been home from the Senate only a few months when he heard that Hardin Runnels was seeking reelection as governor. How could Sam retire? Even if he couldn't control Destiny, he had to lend it a hand. So Sam ran for governor again too. This time he did not wage as strenuous a campaign as he had before; he didn't need to. People had seen that Sam had been right about the Kansas-Nebraska Act, which had not benefited the South at all. Sam made only one speech and referred to himself as an "old fogey" because he still clung to the principles of the Founding Fathers. Over the years he'd been called many names: "The Old Dragon," "Tyrant," "Mr. Eloquent," "Old Humbug," but now except to his bitterest enemies he was simply "Old Sam." People might not agree with him, but when it came time to vote, they found that they loved him anyway. This time they couldn't turn him down.

Sam and his family arrived in Austin in December 1859, ready to move into the three-year-old Governor's Mansion. From the outside the mansion was impressive—a large, tan-colored brick building with dark shutters and six tall white columns that reached from the ground to the roof. Inside there were four rooms downstairs and four bedrooms up-stairs. This had been enough for the first occupants, Governor and Mrs. Pease and their three little girls. It had certainly been enough for Governor Runnels, who was a bachelor and lived alone. But here came the Houstons: Sam and Margaret, Sam, Jr. (sixteen), Nannie (thirteen), Maggie (eleven), Mary Willie (nine), Nettie (seven), Andrew Jackson (five), William Rogers (one), and another Houston on the way. In addition, there were twelve slaves, a nurse, and Sam's secretary. Where would they all fit?

There weren't enough beds for them all. Governor and Mrs. Pease had brought most of their own furniture to the mansion and had taken it with them when they left. Governor Runnels hadn't needed much furniture. And now the legislature was arguing about whether or not it should buy furniture for the mansion. Sam still had enemies, especially in Austin, where people remembered how he had moved the capital away from the city.

A Mr. Mills in the legislature asked why the state should spend money for this governor when it hadn't for the last two? He didn't see why this governor should be treated like a god.

Mr. Culberson made a motion that at least no money should be spent for furniture manufactured in the North.

But Mr. Duncan said it would be "mean" to build a house for the governor and then not furnish it. In the end more members spoke in favor of furnishing the mansion than spoke against it and a bill was passed that provided $1500 for that purpose.

Fortunately, the Houstons didn't have to sit around in their nearly empty house waiting for the government to quit bickering. The committee in charge of preparing the mansion for the new occupants had gone ahead and ordered a new stove, pots and pans, beds, bedding, carpeting, and curtains. An extra bedroom was added by putting up a partition in one of the four upstairs rooms, and when the money was actually approved, more furniture was bought. Perhaps the most impressive piece was Sam Houston's seven-foot-long four-poster mahogany bed, which still stands in the Governor's Mansion.

Even with an extra bedroom, however, the house was crowded—dogs pouring through the hallway, children tearing up and down the stairs, rushing in and out of the house. Young Andrew Jackson was the most active—forever hugging dogs, forever scratching fleabites, forever getting into mischief. Once he locked the door of the senate chamber while the senate was in session. Perhaps his father had taken him to the senate, told him to wait in the hall, and given him the keys to play with. Perhaps Andrew had made his own way down the block to the capitol. In any case, he let the senators know that they were his prisoners. He paid no attention to orders to open the door until his father threatened to whip him and put him in jail. Andrew had undoubtedly been whipped before. But jail? Behind bars? He did as he was told.

Young Andrew's mischief making must have been almost a welcome diversion for Sam, who agonized over how to avoid a civil war that seemed more and more imminent. While he was still in the Senate, Sam had tried to come up with a scheme that would bring the country together. Perhaps Mexico was the answer. Sam had always hankered after Mexico and had persuaded himself that the Mexicans, who couldn't seem to control their own government, would be better off under the United States. Wouldn't it be an act of kindness, Sam asked, for the United States to take over the country and make it a protectorate? In other words, conquer it and share in ruling it. Such a project would bring the North and South together, Sam thought, and stop the terrible secession talk. It would also stop the repeated raids that Mexico was again making into Texas, but the Senate showed no interest.

Sam had sunk his life into the struggle to keep the Union together, however, and he couldn't stop now. Unlike many Southerners who believed they could win a civil war quickly and then go their own way, Sam was a hardheaded realist. He knew that the North had more men, more money, and more power; the South would go down in ruin. *His* South. Texas too. As always, he felt that he and Texas were one. "I made Texas," he said once, and he couldn't bear to look into the future and see Texas humbled and cut down.

Yet there was no denying that the North and the South were teetering on the edge of catastrophe. In October 1859, John Brown heard the voice of God again. This time His orders were to capture the United States arsenal at Harpers Ferry, Virginia (now West Virginia), distribute arms, march south, and free the slaves. The fact that he and twenty-one followers did manage to capture the arsenal and hold it briefly sent the South into a frenzy. What would the Northern abolitionists do next? Would they stop at nothing? And when John Brown was hanged in December, his Northern sympathizers mourned, raged, and vowed that they wouldn't let John Brown die for nothing.

Then South Carolina carried the conflict a step farther. In January 1860, less than a month after Sam's inauguration as governor, the legislature of South Carolina sent a resolution through the South, proclaiming the right of a state to secede from the Union. Of course Sam Houston objected. Indeed, he sounded as fierce as Andrew Jackson speaking out against nullification except that Sam added a plea to people in both the North and the South. He begged them to develop a "brotherly feeling" toward each other. Please, just tend to their own affairs, he said—the North to its way of life, the South to its way.

Sam already had many friends who agreed with him, but this appeal won him more friends. Many of them, fearing war as he did, began promoting him as a candidate for president to be elected in November of that year. Since candidates would be nominated at political conventions to be held in the spring and early summer, it was not too early to bring his name before the public. But when Sam was approached on the subject, he said he would not be a party candidate. He didn't believe in political conventions. All they did was to pit one section of the country against another. All they wanted to do was promote the party itself. They'd promise people anything just to get their votes, and the candidates, if elected, were expected to carry out the promises and give jobs to party favorites. No, Sam said, if he were to be a candidate, he must be nominated not at a convention, not by a political party, but by the people themselves. It was up to them.

On March 2, Sam's sixty-seventh birthday, he bought a boar and a cashmere goat and talked about how many pounds of pork and bacon he ought to be able to sell in a year. A few weeks later he bought Sam, Jr., a white sombrero hat for $4.50. In order to make it fit, Sam said, the hat should be put on first in the cool of the evening after the inside band had been dampened. If Sam Houston was thinking about the presidency, he didn't let on. Still, he wanted it; he'd always wanted it.

And many wanted him to have it. On April 21, at a celebration of the anniversary of San Jacinto, a large crowd of his supporters gathered on the battlefield and nominated him for president of the United States. Sam must have been pleased. He couldn't think of a better place to have his name introduced as a candidate, yet he made no immediate reply. He would wait to see what happened at the conventions.

The first convention was of the Constitutional Union party, a new and rather weak political group, which on May 9 nominated John Bell. Like Houston, Bell was a Union man from the South, and although Houston's name was also proposed, he came in second on the vote. Many were disappointed in the outcome and felt as one New Englander did who said that Houston would have been a stronger candidate. "He has it is true his peculiarities," the New Englander admitted, "but the *people* ... have faith in 'Old Sam.'"

Certainly, the South needed a strong candidate. The next week the Republican party nominated Abraham Lincoln. Actually it didn't matter what Lincoln himself stood for since he was a Republican and so was automatically feared and despised by the South. Lincoln might talk about saving the Union, but Southerners knew that the Republican party was filled with anti-South, anti-slavery men and if Lincoln were elected, the South was doomed.

Sam, fearing war, didn't want Lincoln elected either. He not only longed to be the one to bring peace to a divided nation, he was sure he could do it. So he decided to make a public acceptance of his San Jacinto nomination. He would agree to run as the people's candidate, he announced, but he wanted it understood that he was a *national* candidate, not just a Southern one. He would represent the whole nation, not part of it.

New Yorkers, who had always liked Sam Houston, responded with enthusiasm. On May 29, five days after his announcement, they held a spectacular rally at Union Square, their favorite spot for political demonstrations. Cannon were fired, rockets set off, a brass band played, important speakers praised Sam, and the crowd sang rousing campaign songs. But if Sam had been there, he would have especially liked seeing the huge portrait of himself raised up beside the statue of George Washington.

Sam received encouragement from many parts of the country, but he knew that what the Democrats did at their convention would affect his chances. As it turned out, the Democrats couldn't agree on any candidate and broke up into two factions. The Northern faction nominated Stephen Douglas (whom Sam referred to as "the prince of humbugs") and the Southern faction nominated J. C. Breckinridge, who had been a follower of Calhoun so Sam didn't like him either.

Now there were four candidates running against Lincoln: Bell, Douglas, Breckinridge, and Sam Houston. In other words, with opposition to the Republicans split four ways, no one would have a chance to beat Lincoln. It was a hard fact to face. Yet in the midst of this political disaster, Sam had personal worries too. On August 12 Margaret gave birth to Temple Lea, their fourth son and last child. Margaret, forty-one years old now, had a hard time with this birth and afterward was so sick that Sam did not like to leave her side. For ten nights he didn't even undress, and it was during these sleepless nights that he decided to withdraw his name from the running. Lincoln could not possibly be beaten, he believed, unless his opposition united. Sam must have been disappointed to see this last chance at the presidency slipping away from him, but as usual he did not let on. "Oh, Ben," he wrote a friend, "I forgot to tell you that I am out of the scrape for President. I am arms folded."

Sam's withdrawal did not unite the South, and on November 6, just as Sam had predicted, Abraham Lincoln was elected president. Of course Sam did not—indeed, he could not—sit around with "arms folded." Before the election and after, he pleaded desperately with the South not to do anything rash. "The Union is worth more than Mr. Lincoln," he said. Wait and see, he begged.

But the South was not willing to wait. Although Lincoln would not take office until March, South Carolina seceded from the Union on December 20. Naturally Sam was afraid of what Texas might do. As secessionists stumped the state with their message, Sam stepped up his own efforts. But the mood of the South had changed. There was no laughing, no affectionate talk of "Old Sam" when he appeared now. Indeed, his life was threatened and rocks were once thrown at him. His friends tried to keep him from speaking before unfriendly crowds, but Sam would have none of that. He wasn't going to slink around his own state, but he did make one concession. Under his catskin vest, he carried a pair of pistols.

In January 1861, Southern states began toppling like a row of dominoes, set in motion by South Carolina. First Mississippi, then Florida, Alabama, Georgia, and Louisiana. Jefferson Davis was elected president of the Confederate provisional government and was given as splendid an inauguration as if the South were not on the eve of a war but as if it had already triumphed. Reading the account of the festivities, Sam Houston must have been sick at heart.

"Let me tell you what is coming," he told an audience. "Your fathers and husbands, your sons and brothers, will be herded at the point of a bayonet. You may, after the sacrifice of countless millions, win Southern independence ... but I doubt it."

Secretly he accepted the fact that Texas too would secede, but he had a plan. After secession, why should Texas join the other Confederate states in war? After all, Texas had a destiny of its own. It had made its way alone as an independent republic once, and it could do so again. "Texas has views of expansion," Sam confided in a letter, "not common to many of her sister States ... She will not be content to have the path of her destiny clogged." One way or another, Sam would save Texas, and obviously Mexico was part of his dream.

On February 1 a convention of Texas secessionists voted that the state should secede. Governor Houston protested. What power did the convention think that it had? It had no authority to make legal decisions for a state. Only the people themselves could do that. So it was agreed that on February 23 the people should vote, and as it turned out, they too wanted to secede. There were 46,129 votes in favor of secession, 14,697 that were opposed. On March 4, the day of Lincoln's inauguration, Sam Houston posted a notice on the gate of the capitol announcing the result. He expected that the next steps would be taken by the legislature, which was due to meet on March 18. Then he could introduce his plan for an independent republic.

He never had the chance. The next day the self-appointed convention of secessionists resolved that Texas was now a member of the Confederacy headed by Jefferson Davis.

Sam must have thought that he had already discredited the convention, but here it was, acting again as if Texas had no legal body of its own. How could a convention take over the duties of government? Sam asked. How could it speak for the people? Secession, yes, the people had voted for that, but Confederacy, no. Sam refused to abide by any resolution of a convention. As governor, he had sworn to uphold the constitution, and so far the constitution was unchanged. This group, acting on its own, was annexing Texas to a government the people knew little about, committing it to a constitution that few had ever seen. Sam wrote to the convention, rejecting its authority, and wrote to the secretary of war of the Confederate states, denying that Texas was a member of the Confederacy.

But legal or not, the convention had more power now than Sam Houston had. It did not back down. Instead it announced that all state officials, including the governor, could continue in office on one condition. First, each one must take an oath of allegiance to the Confederacy. Governor Houston was ordered to appear at the capitol at high noon on March 16, 1861.

Sam Houston objected to the illegality of the proceeding more than he objected to joining the Confederacy. Like Andrew Jackson, he was a man who upheld the Constitution and believed in government by the people and by law. In the long run, he wanted to stand by Texas no matter what it decided to do, but the decision should be made according to the established ways of a republican government. All his life he had been faithful to these principles. How could he forsake them now? How could he knuckle under to the dictates of a group of people who had set themselves up as a convention?

Sam knew that there was no use talking. After supper on the night of March 15 he told Margaret that if anyone should call in the evening, he did not want to be disturbed. He went upstairs, took off his coat and vest and shoes, and began pacing the floor. Back and forth he went in his sock feet. Up and down the hall. Across the floor of his bedroom. All night Margaret could hear his footsteps, walking one way as if he were trying out that path, rejecting it, then turning around to try another. But when Sam Houston came down to breakfast, he had reached a decision. "Margaret," he said, "I will never do it."

He went to his office in the basement of the capitol and sat down at his desk. He took out his knife and a piece of soft pine and began to whittle. Upstairs, people were gathering to watch the ceremony. At noon the chairman rapped his gavel on the table. "Sam Houston!" he called. Everyone knew that Sam Houston was not in the room. Yet again his name was called. And then for the third time. "Sam Houston!"

Downstairs, Sam went right on whittling.

The next day, when Sam went to his office, he found the lieutenant governor, a man Sam called "little Eddie" Clark, sitting in his chair. "I presume he must have gotten up before daybreak," Sam said, in order to take possession of the chair.

A few hours later "little Eddie" was sworn in as governor of Texas.

CHAPTER 7

After vacating the Governor's Mansion, the Houston family moved to Cedar Point and had been there less than two weeks when the first shots of the Civil War were fired (April 12). Whatever conflicts Sam had felt about the Union were over now. He was with the Confederacy, and he made this clear in a speech.

"The time has come when a man's section is his country. I stand by mine." For a quarter of a century he had lived, worked, fought, and suffered for Texas and Texans. Now, he said, "I can but cast my lot with theirs, and await the issue."

Within a few months Sam, Jr., had joined the Confederate Army, but none of this—not Sam's own repeated statements nor his son's record—stopped the controversy over Sam Houston. All his life he was loved and hated, attacked and defended (and sometimes still is), but Sam was used to that. What was hard for him was sitting on the sidelines. To his good friend E.W. Cave (former secretary of state, who also had refused to take the oath of allegiance) he confessed that his mind continued to be wrapped up in politics. "I cannot for the life of me," he wrote, "keep from thinking about them."

In October 1862, the Houstons moved from Cedar Point to Huntsville. Sam had long since sold his Raven Hill house and in order to pay his 1857 campaign expenses, he had also sold the Huntsville house. He tried to buy it back, and when he couldn't, he rented a new house, one like no other house in Huntsville or perhaps anywhere else. It didn't even look like a house. The man who built it said he was sick of houses that looked alike so he had modeled this one on a Mississippi River steamboat. It was long and boat-shaped with decks running around both stories and staircases on the outside that flew from one deck to another like a ship's ladders. The front of the house had been turned into a snub-nosed prow, designed, it seemed, to plough through the waves. Queer-looking, people said, but it had an adventurous air as if it were meant for a man who liked to be on the go, even though that man didn't get much farther than the front lawn these days. Sam had a favorite oak tree out there. He'd set his rawhide-bottom chair under that old oak and with his San Jacinto leg propped up on a stool, he looked like a man who, along with his boat, was anchored safely at last in his home port.

He was seventy years old now, ailing, subject to colds, his old war wounds acting up. He could no longer boast that he was hardy as a bear; he was dwindling and he knew it. So in April 1863, he drew up his will, signing it in letters as large as ever, though they trembled in spots. As far as money and property went, he took care of his family in the customary way, but when it came to his children, he couldn't bear to think that he wouldn't be around to give them advice. So he specified that while his sons should be taught English, Latin, Bible, Geography, and History, they should also be taught "an utter contempt for novels and light reading." He left his San Jacinto sword to Sam, Jr., on the provision that it be used only in defense of the Constitution.

In the early days of the war Sam had been heartened by

how well the Southern army did, but like everyone else in the South, when Vicksburg fell, he knew it was only a matter of time before the South fell too. The news of Vicksburg reached Sam on July 7, 1863, and on the next day he came down with a bad cold that developed into pneumonia. It was as if Destiny was playing its last card, sending Sam and the South down together. Three weeks later, on July 26, Sam knew that he was dying. "Margaret," he said. Then drawing his last breath, he whispered, "Texas... Texas." It was as if he should have some last-minute instructions to give his state if he could think what they were or had the strength to say them. It was hard to go away and leave Texas to take care of itself.

But Sam Houston had already given Texas all he had.

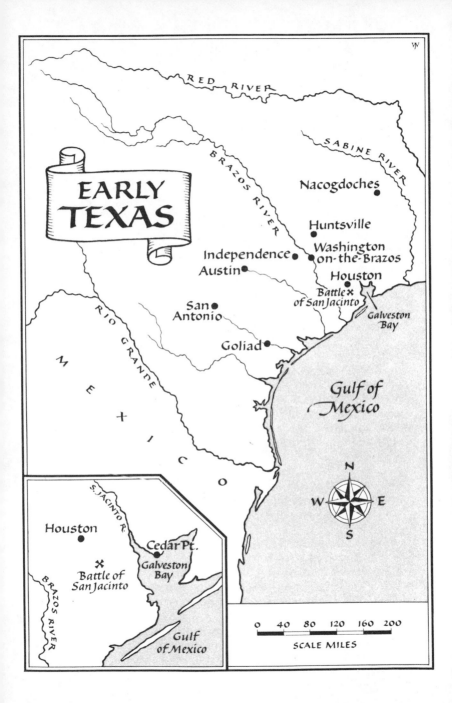

NOTES

Page 13. Montgomery, the capital of Alabama, was named for Major Lemuel P. Montgomery who fell at the Battle of Horseshoe Bend.

Page 15. The Battle of New Orleans was the only major American land victory in the War of 1812, but it was actually fought and won (on January 8, 1815) two weeks after Great Britain and the United States had signed a treaty of peace. The news of the treaty did not reach the United States until after the battle was over. Unnecessary as the battle turned out to be, it was a psychological victory that the Americans very much needed.

Page 22. Although Sam Houston was such a large man, he wore only a size 7 shoe. His mocassins on exhibit at the Sam Houston Memorial Museum in Huntsville look very small indeed.

Page 29. Tiana Rogers was the half sister of John and James Rogers, who had been Sam's best friends in his early days with Chief Jolly's band. She was a thirty-year-old widow when Sam married her. Will Rogers, the "cowboy philosopher" of the 1920s and 1930s, was Tiana's nephew, three generations removed.

Page 29. Indian affairs were managed by the War Department until 1849 when they were transferred to the Department of the Interior. Agents were appointed by the government to manage trade on Indian reservations, but the agents were sometimes corrupt and cheated the Indians. On several occasions Sam Houston intervened and was able to have the corrupt agents removed.

Page 42. It is said that at one point Travis drew a line on the ground and told those who were willing to stay and die with him to cross the line. All crossed except fifty-year-old James Rose, who said he preferred to go on living. He managed to escape and presumably did go on living. The story may or may not be true. It has become part of the Alamo legend, although it has never been authenticated.

Page 45. When Santa Anna and his army were marching through Texas, burning and destroying as they went, the people fled. Their hasty retreat has come to be known as the "Runaway Scrape." The cry would reach a settlement, "The Mexicans are coming!" and everyone would run. The refugees struggled through rainstorms and flood, trying to reach the Louisiana border, and when it was finally safe to return, they found their property in ruins.

Page 45. The Twin Sisters were taken out of Texas during the Civil War, and although Texas has wanted them back, they have never been found.

Page 59. Mirabeau B. Lamar (the "B." stands for Buonoparte) did oil paintings, recited poetry, and was well read. If he was considered a dreamer, he was also known as a cultured gentleman who founded the Philosophical Society of Texas and took important first steps in establishing a system of public education.

Page 68. In a speech in Philadelphia in 1851 Sam boasted how much Texas had improved. "I admit," he said, that Texas was once "a little rude...But now we are becoming an elegant, polite people, of whom I am a fair example." He also pointed out that Texas was the first state to recognize women's property rights. He listed specifically what they were and added, "Now if you can beat that, I will give up."

Page 73. Houston also objected to the Kansas-Nebraska Act because it formed a territory that included land to which the Indians already had title. He made an eloquent plea (as he did again and again throughout his career) for justice to the Indians.

Page 75. Nancy Lea asked to be buried within sound of the church bell and so her grave lies just across the road from the church. The bell rang regularly until a hurricane knocked down the bell tower on March 5, 1969.

Page 78. The people didn't seem to mind how long Sam talked. It was said that there were only two things that could draw a crowd in Texas: a circus and Sam Houston.

Page 84. Houston's enemies were always irritated when he made such remarks as "I made Texas." On January 5, 1861, after he had announced in a speech, "I am the State of Texas," the *Star Gazette* of Austin printed the following comment: "It is to be hoped that he will leave some of his old clothes to the credulous few who yet believe that he is 'the State of Texas.'"

Page 89. After the Texas vote on secession, Lincoln wrote Sam Houston a letter, offering assistance if Houston wished to keep Texas in the Union. Sam did not answer the letter. It is said he threw it in a fireplace at the Governor's Mansion.

Page 92. The Confederates opened fire at Fort Sumter, South Carolina, when the commander of the fort refused to surrender because, he said, it was a federal fort and not subject to the orders of the Confederacy or of South Carolina.

Sam, Jr., was wounded at the Battle of Shiloh in April 1862, and like his father at Horseshoe Bend, was left on the field for dead. A Union chaplain rescued him and he was later returned to his home to recover.

Page 94. The Union army had won the Battle of Gettysburg the day before General Grant took Vicksburg, a turning point in the war, since the Union army now had control of the Mississippi River and the Confederacy was cut in two.

Sam Houston died at 6:15 in the evening. All the clocks at the Sam Houston Memorial Museum in Huntsville stand at 6:15, as if time itself had stopped with Sam Houston. The museum includes the Steamboat House (which has been moved to the present site) and Sam's first Huntsville house (the "bang-up place").

After Sam's death, Margaret moved the family to Independence. In 1867 Margaret died in an epidemic of yellow fever; she is buried in Independence.

BIBLIOGRAPHY

MANUSCRIPTS

Letter from Thomas Goree to his mother, November 20, 1854. Texas Baptist Historical Association. Independence, Texas.

Houston, Sam. Unpublished correspondence. Archives Collection. University of Texas Library. Austin, Texas.

Houston, Sam. Scrapbook. Archives Collection. University of Texas Library. Austin, Texas.

Lamar papers. Archives Collection. Texas State. Austin, Texas.

BOOKS

Carroll, H. Bailey; James M. Day; J. Frank Dobie; Joe B. Frantz; Llerena Friend; Joseph M. Nance; Ben Procter; Rupert N. Richardson; and Dorman H. Winfrey. *Heroes of Texas.* Waco: Texian Press, 1966.

Clarke, Mary Whatley. *Chief Bowles and the Texas Cherokees.* Norman: University of Oklahoma Press, 1971.

Connor, Seymour V.; James M. Day; Joe B. Frantz; Ben Procter; Rupert N. Richardson; Harold B. Simpson; Peck Westmoreland Jr.; and Dorman H. Winfrey. *Battles of Texas.* Waco: Texian Press, 1967.

Crane, William Carey. *Life and Select Literary Remains of Sam Houston of Texas.* Philadelphia: J. B. Lippincott & Co., 1884.

Crawford, Ann, and Crystal Sasse Ragsdale. *Women in Texas.* Austin: Eakin Press, 1982.

Creel, George. *Sam Houston: Colossus in Buckskin*. New York: Cosmopolitan Book Co., 1928.

Day, Donald, and Harry Herbert Ullom, eds. *The Autobiography of Sam Houston*. Norman: University of Oklahoma Press, 1954.

Fehrenbach, T. R. *Lone Star: A History of Texas and Texans*. New York: Macmillan, 1968.

Flanagan, Sue. *Sam Houston's Texas*. Austin: University of Texas Press, 1964.

Foreman, Grant. *Indians and Pioneers: The Story of the American Southwest Before 1838*. New Haven: Yale University Press, 1930.

―――. *Pioneer Days in the Early Southwest*. Cleveland: Arthur H. Clark Co., 1926.

Friend, Llerena. *Sam Houston: The Great Designer*. Austin: University of Texas Press, 1954.

Goetzmann, William H. *When the Eagle Screamed*. New York: John Wiley and Sons, 1966.

Graham, Philip. *The Life and Poems of Mirabeau B. Lamar*. Chapel Hill: University of North Carolina Press, 1938.

Gregory, Jack, and Rennard Strickland. *Sam Houston with the Cherokees, 1829–1833*. Austin: University of Texas Press, 1967.

James, Marquis. *The Life of Andrew Jackson*. New York: Bobbs-Merrill, 1938.

―――. *The Raven: A Biography of Sam Houston*. New York: Blue Ribbon Books, 1929.

Lester, Charles Edward. *The Life of Sam Houston*. New York: J. C. Derby, 1855.

Remini, Robert. *Andrew Jackson and the Course of American Democracy, 1833–1845*. Vol. 3. New York: Harper & Row, 1984.

Richardson, Rupert; Ernest Wallace; and Adrian Anderson. *Texas, the Lone Star State*. New York: Prentice-Hall, 1981.

Ward, John William. *Andrew Jackson: Symbol for an Age*. New York: Oxford University Press, 1953.

Webb, Walter Prescott, and H. Bailey Carroll, eds. *The Handbook of Texas*. Austin: Texas State Historical Society, 1952.

Williams, Amelia M., and Eugene D. Barker, eds. *The Writings of Sam Houston*. 8 vols. Austin: University of Texas Press, 1938–43.

Yoakum, Henderson. *History of Texas, from Its First Settlement in 1685 to Its Annexation to the United States in 1846*. 2 vols. New York: J. S. Redfield, 1855.

ARTICLES

Clark, Joe L. "Sam Houston: Soldier Patriot Man." *East Texas* 2, no. 8 (June 1928).

Harris Dilue. "Reminiscences of Mrs. Dilue Harris." *Quarterly of the Texas State Historical Association* 7 (1903/1904).

Houston, Margaret Lea. "Collected Poems." *The Sam Houston Memorial Museum Quarterly* (Spring 1970).

Littlejohn, E. G. "Some More Houston Stories." *Texas School Journal* (May 1911).

Paschal, George W. "Last Years of Sam Houston." *Harper's New Monthly Magazine* 32 (1865/1866).

Ruffin, Lisa. "Open House: The Governor's Mansion Restored." *Texas Homes* (1982).

Steely, Jim. "The Governor's Mansion." *Texas Highways* (February 1984).

Williams, Amelia. "A Critical Study of the Siege of the Alamo." *Southwestern Historical Quarterly* 37 (October 1933).

Winfrey, Dorman H. "Chief Bowles and the Texas Cherokees." *Texas Military History* (August 1962).

———. "Mirabeau B. Lamar and Texas Nationalism." *Southwestern Historical Quarterly* 59, no. 2 (October 1955).

———. "The Texan Archive War of 1842." *Southwestern Historical Quarterly* (October 1960).

INDEX